SCIENCE
FOUNDATIONS

Global Warming and Climate Change

SCIENCE FOUNDATIONS

SCIENCE
FOUNDATIONS

Global Warming and Climate Change

STEPHEN M. TOMECEK

CHELSEA HOUSE
An Infobase Learning Company

Science Foundations: Global Warming and Climate Change

Copyright © 2012 by Infobase Learning

Chelsea House
An imprint of Infobase Learning
132 West 31st Street
New York, NY 10001

Library of Congress Cataloging-in-Publication Data
Tomecek, Steve.
  Global warming and climate change / Stephen M. Tomecek.
    p. cm. — (Science foundations)
  Includes bibliographical references and index.
  ISBN 978-1-60413-998-3 (hardcover)
  1. Global warming. 2. Climatic changes. I. Title. II. Series.
  QC981.8.G56T66 2011
  363.738'74—dc22   2011006948

Chelsea House books are available at special discounts when purchased in bulk quantities for businesses, associations, institutions, or sales promotions. Please call our Special Sales Department in New York at (212) 967-8800 or (800) 322-8755.

You can find Chelsea House on the World Wide Web at
http://www.infobaselearning.com

Text design by Kerry Casey
Cover design by Alicia Post
Composition by EJB Publishing Services
Cover printed by Yurchak Printing, Landisville, Pa.
Book printed and bound by Yurchak Printing, Landisville, Pa.
Printed in the United States of America

This book is printed on acid-free paper.

All links and Web addresses were checked and verified to be correct at the time of publication. Because of the dynamic nature of the Web, some addresses and links may have changed since publication and may no longer be valid.

Contents

The Mechanics of Weather and Climate

Earth is an ever-changing planet. Over the centuries, forces inside Earth have caused mountains to rise and volcanoes to erupt. Wind and rain acting on the surface have carved out great canyons and worn down mountains to level plains. On a shorter time scale, animals and plants grow and die, the seasons come and go, and weather changes almost every day.

These days you hear quite a bit about Earth's changing climate. It's in the newspapers, on television, online articles, and entire books have been written about it. There is strong evidence that Earth's climate is getting warmer and many scientists believe that humans are to blame. Others claim that the changes are due to natural processes that have operated throughout the planet's history. What follows is a look at climate change and the role that humans may be playing in it. Read the scientific facts and then weigh the evidence for yourself and discover some of the ways that climate change may affect you.

WEATHER VS. CLIMATE

Before taking a look at the causes of climate change, it is necessary to define exactly what climate is. Climate and weather are related.

When scientists talk about the **weather**, they are referring to the current conditions of the **atmosphere** for a specific location on Earth. Some of the factors that are included in weather measurements are air temperature, wind speed and direction, cloud cover, humidity, and precipitation. **Climate** also includes many of these same factors, but instead of focusing on the current conditions for a small area, it is a measure of the average weather conditions over a large region over a much longer period of time. Around the world, climate varies on a regional basis. While weather conditions change on an hourly basis, climate change is usually measured in decades.

Climate change is nothing new. Earth was much colder 15,000 years ago than it is today and the planet was in the grip of a major "ice age." During the Cretaceous Period, 70 million years ago, the average global temperature was several degrees warmer than it currently is. Temperatures are on the rise again. While there is a great debate about the exact cause of this warming trend, most scientists agree that global climate systems are changing.

THE AIR IS THERE

Dozens of factors help to control the climate of a specific region, but in the end it basically comes down to the interaction of heat and moisture in the atmosphere. The make-up of the atmosphere here on Earth is much different than the atmosphere on other planets. Earth's air is a mixture of gases containing many different chemical compounds.

If a "typical" sample of air were dried out so that all of the water vapor were removed, about 99% of the leftover material would be just two gases: nitrogen (N_2) and oxygen (O_2). When people breathe, the nitrogen that goes into the lungs comes back out after it takes a short trip around the circulatory system. It has very little effect on the body, unless you put your body under great pressure, such as when you are scuba diving. Oxygen, on the other hand, is critically important to all living things. Oxygen is used by cells to convert sugar into energy during a process called respiration. Helium, argon, neon, krypton, and xenon are all considered to be *inert* gases. This means that they don't easily combine with other elements. Therefore, like nitrogen, they have little effect on living things.

Table 1.1: Gases in Earth's Atmosphere		
Gas	Symbol	% by Volume (Dry Air)
Nitrogen	N_2	78.084
Oxygen	O_2	20.946
Argon	Ar	0.934
Carbon Dioxide	CO_2	0.033
Neon	Ne	0.00182
Helium	He	0.00053
Krypton	Kr	0.00012
Xenon	Xe	0.00009
Hydrogen	H_2	0.00005
Nitrous Oxide	N_2O	0.00005
Methane	CH_4	0.00002

THE CARBON CYCLE

Even though they make up only a tiny percentage of the atmosphere, two of the most important gases found in the air are carbon dioxide (CO_2) and methane (CH_4). Both contain the element carbon and both are byproducts of chemical processes, including combustion, decomposition, and respiration. Carbon is an important building block of most living things and it is also found in rocks, such as limestone, and in **fossil fuels**, such as coal, oil, and natural gas. Like water, carbon atoms are continuously being passed through different parts of the environment through a natural process called the **carbon cycle**.

The carbon cycle can have an enormous impact on Earth's climate. Here's how it works: During photosynthesis, plants remove carbon dioxide from the air and convert it to sugars in their tissues. Some of these sugars are used by the plants themselves for food in a process called respiration. When this happens, carbon dioxide gas is released back into the air. In other cases, animals eat the plants, or they eat other animals that eat the plants. When they exhale, they also release carbon dioxide into the air. Carbon dioxide also makes its way back into the air when organic material, such as leaves and wood, rot or decompose in the presence of oxygen.

Sometimes carbon gets removed from the carbon cycle and is stored for long periods of time. Trees store an enormous amount of carbon in their wood. As long as they are alive, they keep taking in more. Marine invertebrates, such as corals, make their skeletons from calcium carbonate ($CaCO_3$) and often these get turned into limestone when they die.

Plants and animals don't always decompose quickly. When organic material gets buried under the right conditions, the remains get transformed into coal or oil. When these fossil fuels are burned for energy, carbon dioxide gets released back into the air.

Methane, which is also called "natural gas," gets produced if organic material decomposes when little or no oxygen is present.

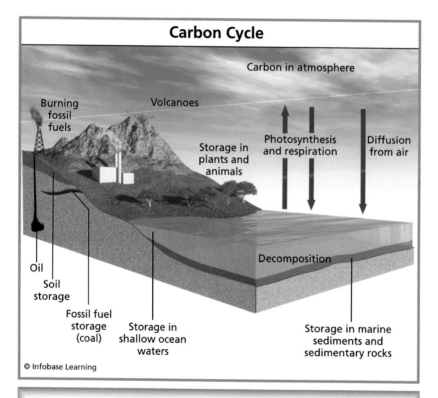

Figure 1.1 Carbon is circulated around Earth in a cycle. It enters seawater from many sources, including air, respiration by living things, erosion of carbon-containing rock, and combustion of fossil fuels. Carbon is removed by processes such as photosynthesis, the creation of limestone, and storage in plants and animals.

This happens in swamps, rice paddies, and inside the stomachs of many animals, such as cows. When the gas is released, it becomes part of the air. Often, methane will get trapped underground or frozen in deposits under the sea and in **permafrost** in the ground. When these deposits thaw out, the methane is released back into the air.

THE STRUCTURE OF THE ATMOSPHERE

People often think of the atmosphere as being a uniform layer of air that surrounds the planet, but this is not the case. Instead, the atmosphere is made up of several different layers marked by changes in temperature. The gases that make up the atmosphere are held in place by Earth's gravity. About half of the total weight of the atmosphere is found within 3.5 miles (5.6 kilometers) of Earth's surface. The boundaries between atmospheric layers are not fixed. They tend to move up and down over time and one layer blends into the next.

The layer of air closest to the ground is called the **troposphere**. There, the air is most dense and turbulent. Almost all the changes that are experienced as "weather" happen in the troposphere. The top of the troposphere varies in height and with latitude being thicker at the equator than at the poles. It averages about 7 miles (11 km) thick. At the equator it is about 11 miles (18 km) thick, while at the poles it is only 5 miles (8 km) thick. Temperature in the troposphere decreases with elevation. That's why it is almost always colder on top of large mountains than in valleys.

At the top of the troposphere, temperatures tend to level off and remain steady. This marks the beginning of the **stratosphere**. The stratosphere extends upward to a height of about 30 miles (48 km) and includes a zone called the **ozone layer**. Once in the ozone layer, the temperatures in the stratosphere begin to steadily increase as elevation increases.

At the top of the stratosphere, temperatures again begin to level off, marking the beginning of the mesosphere. There, the air starts to get extremely cold, with temperatures decreasing with increasing elevation. Roughly 55 miles (88 km) above Earth's surface is the top of the mesosphere. At that point, you reach the thermosphere—the

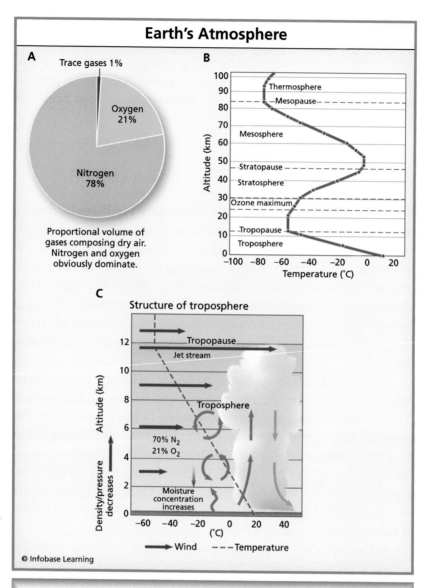

Earth's Atmosphere

A

Trace gases 1%

Oxygen 21%

Nitrogen 78%

Proportional volume of
gases composing dry air.
Nitrogen and oxygen
obviously dominate.

B

Thermosphere
Mesopause
Mesosphere
Stratopause
Stratosphere
Ozone maximum
Tropopause
Troposphere

Altitude (km)

Temperature (°C)

C

Structure of troposphere

Tropopause
Jet stream
Troposphere
70% N$_2$
21% O$_2$
Moisture
concentration
increases

Altitude (km)

Density/pressure decreases

(°C)

→ Wind   --- Temperature

© Infobase Learning

Figure 1.2 (A) Earth's atmosphere is composed of 78% nitrogen, 21% oxygen, and 1% other gases. (B) It is divided into four main layers based on temperature. (C) The troposphere is the layer in which most weather occurs. It averages 7 miles (11 km) high.

uppermost layer of the atmosphere. The thermosphere extends up to about 372 miles (600 km). The area beyond the thermosphere is considered to be space.

A Hole in the Ozone

Ozone is a gas made up of three oxygen atoms joined together (O_3). It is an important part of the atmosphere because this layer helps to block certain types of

(continues)

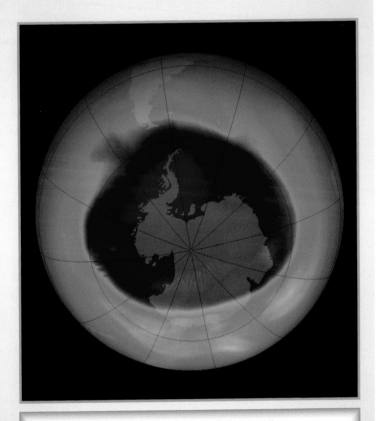

Figure 1.3 Ozone absorbs harmful ultraviolet radiation from the Sun, but its levels are reduced by chlorofluorocarbons and other compounds. This colored satellite image, created with data from the Ozone Monitoring Instrument on the Aura satellite, shows low atmospheric ozone levels over Antarctica on September 11, 2005. The ozone hole (dark blue) is 27 million square kilometers in size. Ozone levels are color-coded, from dark blue (lowest), through cyan and green to yellow (highest).

(continued)

ultraviolet radiation from reaching Earth's surface. Ultraviolet rays are dangerous because repeated exposure can lead to the development of skin cancer and other diseases. Back in the 1970s, atmospheric scientists began noticing that the ozone layer was getting thinner. Things got so bad that an actual hole began opening up over Antarctica each year. It became a matter of great concern because even a small decrease in the ozone layer had the potential to cause big problems for living things on Earth's surface.

After much analysis and quite a bit of controversy, scientists discovered a link between the destruction of the ozone layer and the use of chemicals called chlorofluorocarbons, or CFCs. These compounds were commonly used in air conditioners, in the manufacturing of products such as Styrofoam, and in aerosol cans of hair spray and shaving cream. After CFCs were released near the surface, they drifted up into the stratosphere and began reacting with the ozone, causing it to break down. Something had to be done quickly. In 1987, representatives from 27 nations met and agreed to what has become known as the Montreal Protocol. This document, which was later signed by more than 100 other nations, called for the gradual phasing out and eventual elimination of the use of most CFCs. As of 2009, measurements show that the levels of ozone in the stratosphere have begun to rebound. In some cases, it can take between 75 and 150 years for the CFCs already in the atmosphere to break down. Because of this, a full recovery of the ozone layer may not happen until the twenty-third century.

ENERGY FROM THE SUN

The main force driving all climate patterns on Earth is the Sun. With the exception of a small amount of geothermal energy that originates inside the planet, almost all of the heat on Earth's surface comes from the Sun as **radiant energy,** or radiation. Solar radiation travels through space in the form of electromagnetic waves. The energy carried by these waves does very little until the waves strike an object and are absorbed. You can feel this for yourself on a sunny winter day. If you stand outside and face the Sun, your face will feel warm even though the surrounding air is cold. That's because your skin absorbs some of the solar radiation, which is then transformed into heat energy.

The Sun emits, or gives off, more than one type of radiation. The Sun's radiation comes in a range of waves, each with a different length and amount of energy. Generally speaking, the longer the length of the wave the lower its energy level. Scientists refer to the band of waves coming from the Sun as the **electromagnetic spectrum**. The waves with the longest wavelength are radio waves. After

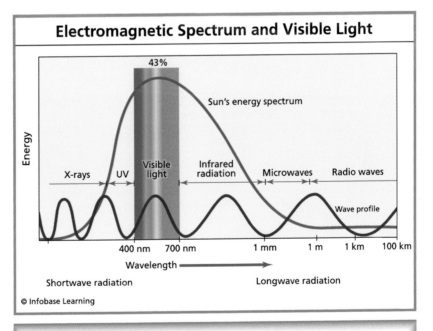

Figure 1.4 The Sun's electromagnetic spectrum ranges from short wavelengths, such as X-rays, to long wavelengths, such as radio waves. The majority of the Sun's energy is concentrated in the visible and near-visible portion of the spectrum, which are the wavelengths located between 400 and 700 nanometers (nm).

radio waves come microwaves, infrared waves (which we commonly call *heat*), visible light (which is the type of waves that we can sense with our eyes), and finally, ultraviolet waves, X-rays, and gamma rays. Gamma rays have extremely short wavelengths and therefore the greatest amount of energy.

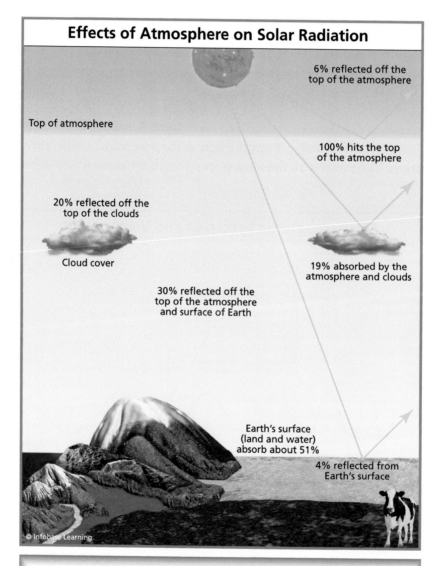

Effects of Atmosphere on Solar Radiation

6% reflected off the top of the atmosphere

Top of atmosphere

100% hits the top of the atmosphere

20% reflected off the top of the clouds

Cloud cover

19% absorbed by the atmosphere and clouds

30% reflected off the top of the atmosphere and surface of Earth

Earth's surface (land and water) absorb about 51%

4% reflected from Earth's surface

© Infobase Learning

Figure 1.5   Only about half (51%) of the solar radiation that strikes the top of the atmosphere is absorbed by Earth. About 30% is reflected back into space and 19% is absorbed by the atmosphere before it reaches the surface of the planet.

When the Sun emits energy, the radiation is not spread evenly over the entire electromagnetic spectrum. More than 95% of the energy is concentrated in the infrared, visible light, and ultraviolet parts of the electromagnetic spectrum. Because of the structure of the atmosphere, only about half (51%) of the Sun's radiation is absorbed by Earth's surface. About 30% is reflected by clouds, water, ice, and the land's surface itself. Another 19% is absorbed by clouds and the gases that make up the air.

Most of the infrared and ultraviolet radiation that hits the top of the atmosphere never gets through to Earth's surface. Instead it is either absorbed by the upper atmosphere or gets reflected back into space. The part of the electromagnetic spectrum that does make it through is mostly visible light. When visible light waves strike Earth's surface they are either reflected or absorbed. It is the absorbed light waves that heat the surface of the planet. Some of this heat energy is then re-radiated, or sent, back into space as infrared radiation, heating the air in the lower atmosphere from the bottom up. This explains why the air gets cooler in higher elevations. The Sun doesn't heat the air directly. It heats Earth, and Earth heats the air.

THE GREENHOUSE EFFECT

One of the most important factors controlling Earth's surface temperature is the **greenhouse effect**. This phenomenon explains how certain gases in the atmosphere absorb infrared radiation and help hold heat near the planet's surface. The name comes from the way that the glass in a florist's greenhouse helps to trap heat on the inside of the building, even during cold winter days. In a typical greenhouse, solar radiation in the form of visible light enters through the glass and is absorbed by the objects inside. The energy is then re-radiated at longer infrared wavelengths inside the building. While the glass is transparent to visible light waves, it tends to block the longer infrared waves and keeps them from passing back outside.

In the lower atmosphere, gases such as water vapor (H_2O), carbon dioxide (CO_2), methane (CH_4), and nitrous oxide (N_2O) are all strong absorbers of infrared radiation, but they are mostly transparent to visible light. As previously noted, when visible light hits

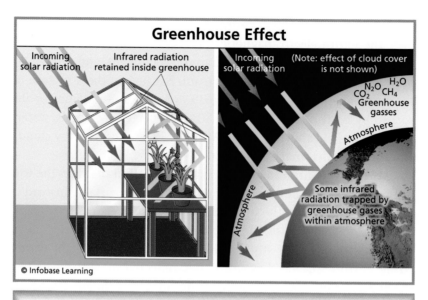

Figure 1.6 Gases in the atmosphere, called greenhouse gases, stop some solar radiation from escaping into space. The natural process between the Sun, the atmosphere and Earth is called the greenhouse effect because it works the same way as a greenhouse.

Earth's surface, it is reflected as infrared radiation and is absorbed by these gases. The gases then slowly release the heat back into the atmosphere, keeping Earth's average surface temperature around 59°F (15°C). Without this atmospheric greenhouse effect, the average surface temperature of the planet would be only about 0°F (-18°C). Many life forms would find it difficult to survive.

Problems happen when the greenhouse effect becomes too great and the temperature continues to rise. This is the case on Venus, which has a runaway greenhouse effect. Because Venus's atmosphere is dominated by carbon dioxide gas, the daytime surface temperature of the planet is more than 850°F (454°C).

EARTH'S ENERGY BALANCE

If it were not for the atmospheric greenhouse effect, Earth would be in a deep freeze. The make-up of Earth's atmosphere plays an important role in maintaining the average surface temperature of the planet, but it is not the only factor controlling the temperature of Earth's surface. In order to get the big picture of how average global surface temperature can change over time, atmospheric scientists look at something called Earth's *energy balance*. This can be thought of as a type of bank account—but instead of money, the account contains energy. Here's how it works:

In order for the planet's average annual surface temperature to remain constant, Earth must release the same amount of energy back into space as it receives from the Sun. In other words, the energy additions must equal the energy subtractions in order for the total to stay in balance. When sunlight strikes the atmosphere, a number of important interactions take place. Some of the radiation is absorbed by gases in the air, but when light hits dust and air molecules, it also gets scattered. Air molecules tend to scatter the shorter (blue) wavelengths of light more than the longer (red) ones, which is the primary reason the sky looks blue.

When light rays are scattered, they tend to be deflected in all directions. When light rays bounce off objects in the direction from which they came, they are said to be *reflected*. Dust, volcanic

Average Global Surface Temperature

Average global surface temperature is the average temperature of the air and water of Earth's entire surface for a selected period of time, such as a month or a year. It is calculated using data from several thousand weather stations around the world, in addition to sea surface temperatures taken from satellite measurements. Using this data, scientists create large-scale maps showing how temperatures change over the entire world on a monthly or yearly basis. Because it is an average, in some places the local surface temperatures could be going down even if the global average is going up.

Table 1.2: Albedo Numbers Based on Surfaces	
Type of Surface	Albedo
Fresh Snow	75% to 95%
Ice	30% to 40%
Sand	15% to 45%
Grassy Field	10% to 30%
Dry Plowed Field	5% to 20%
Water	10%
Forest	3% to 10%

ash, and tiny particles produced by smoke and air pollution can also reflect solar radiation back into space. Scientists measure the relative reflectivity of an object by calculating its **albedo.** The albedo of an object is the percentage of the incoming radiation that is reflected off its surface. In general, objects with a darker, duller surface have a lower albedo than those with a light-colored, shiny surface. Thick clouds have a very high albedo, often reaching as much as 90%. As clouds get thinner, the albedo decreases to a low of about 30%.

Objects in the air are not the only things that reflect sunlight. Earth's surface can also cause solar radiation to bounce off and return to space. Snow, ice, water, and even rocks all have an effect on the overall energy balance. Because each of these materials has a different albedo, changes in how land is used can play a major role in changing Earth's energy balance.

CHANGES IN THE ENERGY BALANCE

In order for Earth's surface temperature to remain constant, the overall energy balance also has to remain steady. Over the years scientists have identified a number of variables that can change the energy balance of the planet. Some involve changes on Earth's surface and others involve changes in the make-up of the atmosphere. One of the most important variables has to do with the amount of sunlight that reaches Earth from the sun.

Changes in Solar Radiation

The Sun might seem like a big ball of burning gas, but the truth is that it is not really on fire. The Sun produces radiant energy by means of a process called nuclear fusion. During this reaction hydrogen atoms are converted into helium atoms at an enormous rate. As a result, the amount of energy that the Sun releases into space as radiation does vary, but it stays within a fairly narrow range. When scientists calculate Earth's energy balance, they generally use a fixed number called the **solar constant** for the amount of solar radiation striking the top of the atmosphere.

The amount of energy reaching Earth does change over time because of changes in its orbit. Earth's orbit around the Sun is not a perfect circle. Instead, it is an ellipse, or oval. During the course of the year there are times when Earth is closer to the Sun (a point called perihelion) and farther away (aphelion). At perihelion, which currently falls around January 2, Earth gets slightly more radiation then it does at aphelion.

Astronomers have discovered that there are several other cycles that have a long-term effect on the amount of solar radiation that the planet receives. Even though Earth's current orbit is an ellipse, it is fairly close to being a circle. Over time the orbit tends to get more stretched out and then becomes circular again. This cycle lasts about 100,000 years. The more elliptical the orbit is, the greater the variation in solar energy Earth receives during the year.

Another cycle has to do with the tilt of Earth's axis of rotation. It is this tilted axis that is responsible for Earth's seasons. Right now, Earth's axis is tilted at an angle of about 23.5°. This angle slowly changes over a 41,000-year period, with the maximum tilt being about 24° and the minimum around 22°. The larger the angle of tilt, the bigger the difference between winter and summer temperatures on the planet.

Precession, the final cycle dealing with Earth's orbit, also has to do with the tilt of the planet's axis. Instead of controlling how large the tilt is, precession controls the direction in which the axis is pointed. This in turn controls the time of the year that each hemisphere has winter and summer. If you have ever watched a spinning top, you've probably noticed that as the top slows down, the axis begins to wobble in a small circle. This same thing is happening to Earth when it rotates. Right now, the top of Earth's axis is pointed directly at the North Star, otherwise known as Polaris. Over time, it will gradually turn and point in the opposite direction toward a star called Vega. Then it will point back to Polaris again. The cycle of precession takes about 26,000 years to complete.

Individually, each one of these orbital cycles has only a small effect on the amount of solar radiation hitting Earth. Because each cycle runs on a different period of time, over the course of thousands of years there are times when the effects of each cycle overlap, and either add together or cancel each other out. After doing detailed studies of these cycles, a number of scientists have concluded that, taken together, these changes in Earth's orbit can have a major impact on the amount of solar radiation the planet receives. Some scientists believe that they are at least partially responsible for controlling the ice ages that the planet has experienced over the last 2 million years.

Changes in the Atmosphere

When conditions in the atmosphere change, they can have a major impact on Earth's energy balance. Most of the atmosphere is made up of invisible gases, but there is also a significant amount of microscopic drops of liquid and solid particles called **aerosols** present in the air. Depending on how high they are in the atmosphere and what they are made of, they can either increase the amount of heat trapped in the air, or cool the planet by reflecting more sunlight back into space.

Aerosols can be naturally occurring or man-made. The biggest source of natural aerosols is volcanoes. When certain types of volcanoes erupt, they produce an enormous amount of tiny ash particles and sulfur compounds, which can easily reach the stratosphere. The solid ash particles are highly reflective and help to reduce the amount of incoming solar radiation by reflecting it back into space. Over time, the sulfur compounds found in the volcanic gases combine with water vapor to form tiny droplets of sulfuric acid. These are also highly reflective.

Natural aerosols in the stratosphere can have a really chilling effect on Earth. In June 1991, Mt. Pinatubo in the Philippines underwent a series of large eruptions, resulting in thick clouds of ash and gas reaching the stratosphere. Winds quickly spread the aerosols around the planet. This reduced the amount of solar radiation that reached the surface. Temperature records show that by July 1992, Earth's surface temperature had dropped by almost a full degree (0.9°F or 0.5°C). This was not the first time in recorded history that volcanic aerosols cooled Earth. Following the massive eruption of Mt. Tambora in Indonesia in 1815, temperatures dropped so much in North America and Europe that 1816 became known as "the year without a summer."

Aerosols don't always reach the stratosphere. Often, they only get into the troposphere, where their effect on solar radiation is a little less understood. Dust from wind storms and low-level volcanic ash also tend to reflect sunlight back into space. Soot and smoke from wildfires tend to absorb sunlight, which in turn heats up the lower atmosphere. The largest source of man-made aerosols comes from the burning of coal in factories and power plants, and from vehicle exhaust. These compounds mix with water vapor to form a thick haze called *smog*. During the daytime, smog will reflect sunlight back into space, cooling the surface. At night, it acts like a blanket, trapping heat near Earth's surface. A great deal of research still has to happen before scientists fully understand the role that man-made aerosols play in climate change.

Aerosols aren't the only substance in the atmosphere that can change the planet's energy balance. Some of the gases that make up the atmosphere—such as carbon dioxide, methane, nitrous oxide, and water vapor—are considered to be **greenhouse gases**. One of the biggest concerns that atmospheric scientists have is how increases in the concentration of these gases affect the surface temperature of the planet. During the past 200 years the concentration of carbon dioxide in the atmosphere has steadily increased. Climate data for the last century show that Earth's average surface temperature has also been steadily increasing. Many scientists believe that there is a definite link between the two. This link will be discussed in detail in Chapter 3.

Changes in Land Use

Over the last half-century, large sections of rainforest in South America, Central America, and Indonesia have been cleared to make room for farms, ranches, and other development. Tropical rain forests aren't the only places where changes in land use are happening. Changes are also occurring in industrialized nations. *Urban sprawl* is a term that scientists use to describe the outward movement of cities into the surrounding rural areas. It's easy to see

The Keeling Curve

During the mid-1900s, a growing number of scientists began wondering what effect, if any, the burning of fossil fuels had on the concentration of carbon dioxide in the atmosphere. Many scientists just assumed that any additional CO_2 that went into the air would simply be absorbed by the oceans and that the concentration in the air would remain fairly steady. The problem was that there was no real way of accurately measuring the balance of different gases in the atmosphere.

Charles David Keeling didn't like assumptions. In 1953, Keeling was working as a postdoctoral fellow in geochemistry at the California Institute of Technology. For three years, he developed a system for measuring tiny changes in the CO_2 concentration of the air. He began collecting data showing that, outside of cities and forests, the concentration of CO_2 in the atmosphere was fairly constant all over the planet. This value is now called the atmospheric background of carbon dioxide.

In 1958, with the support of the U.S. Weather Service, Keeling set up a monitoring station at the Mauna Loa Observatory in Hawaii, which is on top of an extinct volcano reaching 11,135 feet (3,400 m) in height. There, far from sources of air pollution, he began taking detailed measurements of the CO_2 background in the air. At the time he found that the concentration was 310 parts per million (ppm). He continued taking measurements during the next 45 years and what he saw confirmed the worst fears of climate scientists. The oceans were indeed absorbing some of the extra CO_2, but not all of it. During Keeling's studies the atmospheric background of CO_2 steadily increased. Today it how urban sprawl could develop. In an effort to get away from the crowded cities, people began to push outward, creating suburbs.

The construction of new houses, roads, schools, and shopping malls means that land that was once covered by grass and trees is paved over with concrete and asphalt. If you've ever stepped on

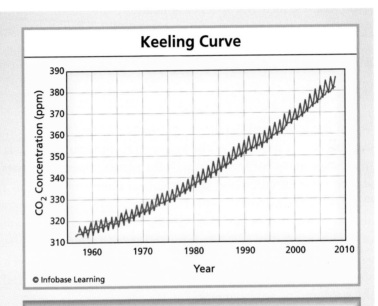

© Infobase Learning

Figure 1.7 Since the first information was collected for it 1958, the Keeling Curve has been instrumental in providing evidence that CO_2 levels are rising worldwide. In the curve, the blue line depicts readings collected from the Mauna Loa observation station, and the red line depicts data collected from the South Pole.

stands at 388 ppm. What's worse is that as more fossil fuels are burned, the rate of increase is accelerating. Some scientists estimate that if the trend continues, CO_2 level of 500 ppm or more may be common by the end of the century.

Charles Keeling died in 2005. His son Ralph, who is also an atmospheric scientist, is continuing his work. Keeling will always be remembered for his groundbreaking work. The plot of the data he collected is known by climate scientists around the world as the *Keeling Curve*.

pavement in bare feet on a bright, sunny day, you know that it gets exceptionally hot. Materials such as concrete and asphalt absorb sunlight and re-radiate it as heat much more efficiently than grass, trees, and soil. During the day, air temperatures around paved areas soar, while near grass and trees they stay relatively cool. In addition, a mass of concrete helps to store heat, so once the sun sets, the air around paved areas stays warmer for a longer period of time. Scientists call these local hot spots **heat islands**.

INTERACTIONS OF LAND, AIR, AND WATER

When it comes to understanding climate change, Earth's total energy balance is only part of the picture. Of equal importance is how the energy gets distributed around the planet. Different substances absorb solar radiation and store the heat energy at different rates. One way of comparing the effects of heat energy on different materials is to measure **specific heat**. Specific heat is defined as the amount of energy needed to raise the temperature of 1 gram of a particular substance by 1 degree Celsius. Specific heat controls how fast a substance heats up and then how quickly the energy is re-radiated into the surrounding environment.

Liquid water has one of the highest specific heat values of any common substance—almost five times greater than rock, dry soil, and dry sand. To understand why this is important, all you need to do is visit a sandy beach near a pond on a sunny day. Early in the morning, the sand on the beach is generally cooler than the water. After a few hours in the sun, the sand starts to warm up, but the water remains cool because it takes five times more solar energy to heat it to the same temperature. When the evening rolls around, the sand cools off quickly because it has a low specific heat. The water, which has taken all day to warm up, stays warm well into the night because it loses heat more slowly.

Because of water's high specific heat, the ocean acts as an important "heat sink" for the planet by helping to even out the local air temperature. On hot days the water absorbs heat energy from the air while slowly rising in temperature. On cold days (or at night) the water releases the stored energy back into the atmosphere, helping to warm the surrounding air. Since almost 70% of Earth is covered by oceans, the role that water plays in controlling and stabilizing climates is huge. Even small changes in the temperature of the ocean can have enormous impacts on climates around the globe.

MOVEMENT OF AIR AND WATER

If you have ever walked around on a windy day or swum in the ocean where there is a strong current, you know first hand about the movement of air and water. This movement not only affects local weather patterns, but it also helps to control the different climates found on Earth. To understand how this happens, one must learn about the physics of air and water, and how these two substances behave when their temperatures change.

By definition, both air (a gas) and water (a liquid) are classified as fluids. A **fluid** is any form of matter that will naturally flow from one place to another when it encounters a force such as gravity. It is easy to understand the fluid nature of water because it is visible. Because air is usually invisible, its fluid nature is a little more difficult to understand, but the two behave pretty much in the same way.

The reason that Earth's atmosphere is thickest near the surface is that the air molecules are being pulled down toward the planet by gravity. However, gravity isn't the only force that affects the motion of fluids. They are also controlled by heat. When fluids get hot, they generally increase in volume, or expand. This happens because the fluid's molecules vibrate faster and literally push each other apart. When fluids expand, they become less dense. Density is a measure of how much matter takes up how much space. Its mathematical formula is density = mass ÷volume.

CONVECTION CURRENTS IN AIR AND WATER

When fluids get warm, they do not heat up evenly. The portion of the fluid closest to the heat source gets hot faster and begins to expand faster than the surrounding fluid. As a fluid expands, it becomes less dense and begins to get pushed up by the surrounding fluid, which is denser and cooler. As the warm fluid continues to move away from the heat, it begins to cool down again and its density increases. This causes the fluid to flow back toward the heat, making a large, loop-shaped pattern called a **convection** current.

You can see a convection current by following the bubbles in a clear glass pot of boiling water on a stove. First, the bubbles will rise up in the center, from the bottom of the pot toward the top. Then they will spread out across the top to the sides of the pot, and finally

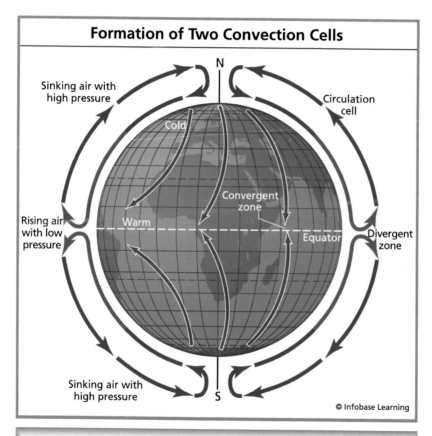

Figure 1.8 In this simplistic view of how convention cells affect Earth, the warm, light air at the equator rises and spreads northward and southward, and the cool, dense air at the poles sinks and spreads toward the equator, forming two convention cells.

they will begin to sink back down toward the bottom along the edges of the pot, where it is cooler.

Convection currents are thought to be responsible for the motion of many things in nature, including the tectonic plates that make up Earth's crust and the winds that blow in the air above it. The Sun doesn't heat the air in the lower atmosphere directly. Instead, the air is heated by Earth's surface after it has absorbed radiation from the Sun. This means that under normal circumstances, during the day the air flows up from the surface toward higher levels in the atmosphere, and there is an updraft. Because the cooler air to the sides of the updraft is denser than the warm air inside of it, the cool air pushes harder against the surface than the warm air does. In other words, the air pressure of the cool air tends to be greater than the warm air.

Fluids always flow from areas of high pressure to areas of low pressure. Wind is, in fact, air flowing horizontally from a high-pressure area to fill in the space left by the rising air in a low-pressure zone. Areas where flowing air come together are called *convergent*

Sea Breeze vs. Land Breeze

One of the interesting things about wind is that in areas along the ocean or large lakes, it will periodically shift directions during the day. This happens because of unequal heating of the air by two different sources at different times of the day. During the day, the land surface heats up much faster than the water because it has a lower specific heat. This causes the air above the land to heat faster than the air over the water. As the air over the land rises, air rushes in from the area over the water, bringing in a cool sea breeze. (Winds are always named for the direction from which they come.) At night, the land cools off faster than the water, and eventually comes the point at which the air over the water is warmer than the air over the land. This causes the convection cell to reverse direction, creating a land breeze blowing out over the water.

zones. Places where the air flows apart are called *divergent zones.* These two zones always come in pairs. There can't be a convergent zone without a divergent zone. If there is a convergent zone at the surface, then there must be a corresponding divergent zone higher in the atmosphere above it.

THE CORIOLIS EFFECT

If the only factor affecting the motion of air and water on the planet were density due to unequal heating and cooling, then predicting weather and changes in climate would be relatively easy. Unfortunately nature is much more complex, and it often throws scientists a few curves. One of the biggest curves has to do with the **Coriolis effect**. Instead of following a straight path, fluids moving on and above Earth's surface are deflected and tend to follow a curved path instead. This happens because Earth is rotating. What's interesting is that the direction of the deflection in the Northern Hemisphere is opposite that of the Southern Hemisphere. This is due to the fact that the planet spins fastest at the equator and slows toward the two poles. In the Northern Hemisphere, winds will tend to flow in a clockwise direction, out from areas of high pressure, and spin counter-clockwise in toward low-pressure zones. In the Southern Hemisphere, the patterns reverse. In a similar manner, ocean currents in the Northern Hemisphere flow in a clockwise direction, and in a counter-clockwise direction south of the equator.

GLOBAL WIND BELTS

Local winds can form and change direction as a result of unequal heating and cooling of air by Earth's surface. This same process happens on a much larger scale in the atmosphere as a whole. The result is a series of wind belts that circle the globe at different latitudes.

Because Earth is round, when sunlight hits the planet the amount of energy is not evenly distributed. More direct sunlight strikes Earth near the equator than at the poles. That's why the tropics are always warm and the poles are always cold. As a result, the air above the equator gets heated more than the air above the poles. As the warm air above the equator rises up into the atmosphere, it begins to split apart and flow north and south. In other words, at the equator there is a divergent zone high in the atmosphere. Cooler air from the north and south flows in at the surface to fill the space, creating a convergent zone there. This area of low pressure at the equator is called the *inter-tropical convergence zone*, or ITCZ for short.

Instead of moving directly north and south, the winds are turned by the Coriolis effect. The winds flowing toward the equator in the Northern Hemisphere come from the northeast, and those in the Southern Hemisphere flow from the southeast. As the air in the upper atmosphere moves away from the equator and toward the poles, it is cooled and becomes denser. It begins to sink back down toward the surface at 30 degrees north and south latitude creating a zone with little or no surface wind. These areas are known as the *horse latitudes* because in the past, sailing ships would often become stranded here for weeks. Food and fresh water would become scarce and the men were often forced to either eat their horses, or throw them overboard. When the sinking air reaches the surface at the horse latitudes, it creates two high-pressure zones called the *subtropical highs*. It also creates another set of divergent zones. This same process of alternating convergent and divergent zones is repeated at 60 degrees north and south latitude and again at the poles. As a result, Earth has a rather complex pattern of global wind belts that play a direct role in controlling weather and climate patterns on the planet.

THE MOTION IN THE OCEAN

Like the air in the atmosphere, the water found in the world's oceans is in constant motion. In addition to waves and tides, currents found on both the surface and at different ocean depths move large volumes of seawater around the planet. Most of the major surface currents on Earth are linked to the global wind belts. When the air flows over the surface of the sea, it pushes the water along with it. Because water is much denser than air, the speed of the ocean currents is much slower than the winds.

Even though the winds start the ocean currents moving, they are not the only factor controlling the direction of flow. Land masses and the topography of the sea floor also help to channel the flow. In addition, temperature and density differences found in the water can impact how the water moves. Apart from the wind, the biggest factor controlling the direction of surface currents is the Coriolis effect. Earth's rotation causes the different ocean currents to form large circular gyres that spiral in different directions. As a result, in the Northern Hemisphere the surface currents tend to move in a clockwise direction, while in the Southern Hemisphere they move counter-clockwise.

CLIMATE ZONES ON EARTH

Earth does not have one uniform climate. A number of different factors, including the intensity and duration of sunlight, the distribution of land and water, and the direction of the wind all interact with each other to create different climate zones. Some of the other factors that play an important role in the creation of a particular climate zone are the amount of urbanization, the elevation of the area, and whether there are any natural barriers to the movement of air, such as tall mountains or deep valleys.

The main factor controlling the temperature of a particular area is the sunlight. Generally speaking, the temperature is warmer closer to the equator. This is because more direct radiation from the Sun strikes Earth near the equator than at the poles. Another factor controlling temperature is elevation. The higher the elevation, the colder the temperature tends to be.

There are exceptions to these simple rules, though. Take Scotland, for example. It has the same approximate latitude as northern Canada. Based on this fact alone, a person might assume that Scotland would have a cold winter climate, but that's incorrect. The normal temperature along the Scottish coast is quite a bit warmer than the temperature in northern Canada. The reason for this surprising temperature difference is the flow of the Gulf Stream.

The Gulf Stream can be thought of as a large river flowing right through the ocean. This warm water current was first reported by the explorer Ponce de Leon back in the early 1500s, and it was extensively studied by Benjamin Franklin. The Gulf Stream starts off as the Florida Current in the tropical Atlantic, where it picks up a tremendous amount of heat energy from the Sun. It then flows northeast along the coast of North America, going all the way up to the Grand Banks of Newfoundland in Canada. The current then takes a turn toward the east and heads across the Atlantic Ocean as the North Atlantic Drift.

Eventually the warm water reaches the coasts of Scotland and Norway, where it creates an unusually warm **microclimate**. Meanwhile, on the western side of the Atlantic, the Labrador Current carries extremely cold water down from the arctic and along the coast of Northern Canada, flowing in behind the Gulf Stream. This cold water current provides a major chilling effect along the Canadian coast.

Ocean currents aren't the only geographic feature that can affect a local climate. When it comes to climates in the interior areas of continents, mountains play a huge role in stopping the flow of moisture. A great example of this can be seen along the West Coast of the United States. Air moving from the Pacific Ocean toward the land usually has a great deal of moisture in it. When this humid air moves across the land, it encounters the Coast Range Mountains. As the air moves up and over the mountains, it begins to cool, which causes precipitation on the windward side of the mountains. Once the air moves down the opposite side of the mountains (called the leeward side) it has lost a great deal of moisture.

The air continues to move east across the Central Valley and then hits the even higher Sierra Nevada mountain range. This second uplift causes most of the remaining moisture to fall out of the air, so by the time it reaches the leeward side of the Sierras, the air is extremely dry. The result is that much of the state of Nevada is a desert. This type of desert is called a *rain shadow desert*. They can be found all over the world.

In an effort to sort out all the different climatic differences around the world, scientists have come up with several different ways of classifying them. For the most part, each of these schemes covers the same general climate factors, focusing primarily on temperature and humidity. One of the most widely used classification systems was first developed in 1918 by German scientist Wladimir Köppen. It is still referred to as the Köppen System. Köppen realized that certain types of vegetation would only grow under very specific temperature and moisture conditions. Using patterns of vegetation as the key, he defined the following five major global climate types:

- Tropical moist climates
- Dry climates
- Moist mid-latitude climates with mild winters
- Moist mid-latitude climates with severe winters
- Polar climates

Each of these major climate types contains numerous sub-regions with special characteristics, including the effects of elevation. Over the years the Köppen System has been modified to better fit climate data. It has proven to be particularly useful to scientists who study how regional climates have shifted over time.

Over the past century, scientists have noticed that the vegetation that defines each climate zone has shifted its position. This, along with temperature and precipitation records from around the globe, has strongly suggested that Earth's overall climate has been changing. Most scientists agree that during the past century the surface temperature of the planet has gotten warmer. The question is, have these types of changes happened in the past and, if so, what has caused them to occur? To understand how the current levels of climate change fit into the big picture, it is first necessary to take a look at Earth's climate in the past.

Earth's History of Climate Change

Based on the geological record, scientists know that the climate of the planet has changed quite a bit during its 4.6 billion-year history. The study of ancient climates based on rock formations and fossils is called **paleoclimatology**. The principles behind it are really quite simple. It's based on the idea that the present is the key to the past.

Here's how paleoclimatology works: Let's say that you find a layer of salt sandwiched between two layers of sandstone. If you go to places in the world where salt crystals are forming today (the present), you would find that they occur only in areas that have warm and dry climates, such as in the Middle East. Using this information, you can assume that when the layer of salt formed in the ancient rocks (the past), the climate during that time at that location was also warm and dry.

Over the years geologists have identified numerous types of clues to ancient climates, including plant and animal fossils, coal deposits, sand dunes, and deposits left by glaciers. Using these methods they have slowly pieced together a long climate history for the planet.

There is, however, a catch. Not only has Earth's climate changed over time, but so has the position of its rocks. According to plate tectonic theory, all of the present-day continents have slowly changed their positions on the globe over time. If this is the case (and most geologists believe it is true), then the question remains: What really changed—the climate or the location of the rocks?

An example of this can be seen in Antarctica. Fossils in rocks there show that the continent once had a tropical climate. Based on this evidence alone, it would seem that Earth must have been much warmer in the past. That, however, assumes that the landmass called Antarctica was always sitting at the South Pole. Based on other evidence, geologists believe that it wasn't. In fact, they are pretty certain that Antarctica was sitting right near the equator at one point in the past, which would explain the tropical climate better than massive global warming.

Figure 2.1   Earth's southernmost continent, Antarctica, is approximately 98% covered by ice that is about 1 mile (1.6 km) thick on average. Today, it is home to many cold-adapted plants and animals, including penguins, but it had a tropical climate in the distant past.

Such a dynamic planet has caused quite a dilemma for people who wish to study it. Fortunately, by working together, geologists and paleoclimatologists have been able to sort out enough of the data to show that during the past, Earth has indeed gone through some huge climate changes. The most famous of these is commonly called the *ice age*.

LONG-TERM CLIMATE CHANGES

When most people hear the term *ice age*, a desolate ice-covered world with giant mammoths roaming around the tundra usually comes to mind. Although these images are accurate to some extent, there are a few important points that must be made.

First, the term *ice age* refers to several different ice ages. There have been many of them during Earth's history. The last ice age, or **glacial period**, as they are technically called, ended between 12,000 and 15,000 years ago. During the last 2 million years (a period called the Pleistocene Epoch), there have been at least four major glacial periods separated by relatively warm periods, known as an **interglacial stage**. In fact, some scientists believe that the warm period that we have been experiencing during the last 12,000 years is really nothing more than another interglacial stage.

The second mistake people make about glacial periods is to think that all of Earth was covered by ice. During the last glacial stage (known as the *Wisconsin Glacial Stage* in North America), the maximum extent of ice in the Northern Hemisphere was from the North Pole to around 40 degrees north latitude. Although this is a huge amount of ice, it also means that more than two-thirds of the Earth was still ice-free.

Using several lines of evidence, scientists have estimated that the last glacial stage began when the global temperature dropped by about 5°C (9°F). This change may not sound like much, but it shows just how delicate the balance is between global temperature and climate. The question is, what caused Earth to cool down and then mysteriously warm up again? Could this same process be what is causing the warming that Earth is experiencing today? There is still a great deal of debate about the exact mechanism that triggered

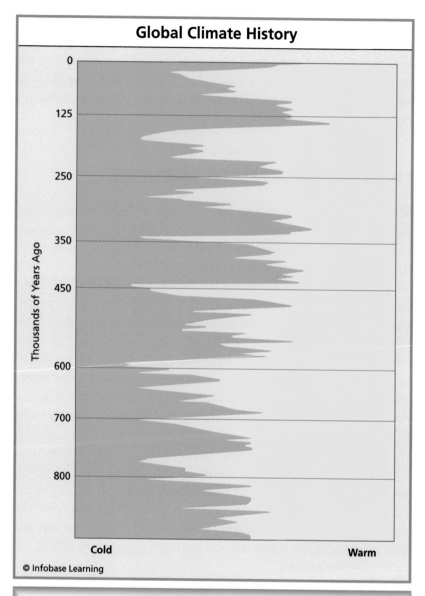

Global Climate History

Thousands of Years Ago

0
125
250
350
450
600
700
800

Cold   Warm

© Infobase Learning

Figure 2.2 This graph illustrates how climate has varied from hot to cold over time.

the spread of glaciers during the Pleistocene Epoch. Even so, there is growing support among scientists for the idea that Earth's orbit around the Sun is the key to the glacial cycles.

As explained earlier, variations in the shape of Earth's orbit and the tilt of the axis can have an impact on the amount of solar radiation that the planet receives. Individual factors, such as the angle of tilt, the shape of the orbit, and the wobble of the axis each have minimal effects on the amount of solar energy that strikes Earth's surface. But what if these different factors were added together? Back in the early 1900s, Yugoslavian astronomer Milutin Milankovitch asked this very question. The answer he came up with was quite surprising.

Milankovitch wasn't the first person to suggest that variations in the amount of solar energy played a role in the glacial-interglacial cycles, but he was the first to actually plot out all the data to see if they matched their timing. Based on his findings, he came up with a theory that explained the cyclic nature of the Pleistocene ice ages. He showed how the three orbital cycles would periodically align to produce conditions in which temperatures in the Northern Hemisphere would remain quite cold, even during the summer months. Under these conditions, snow that fell during the winter months would never completely melt. Over the course of several years, these annual snow layers gradually built up. They eventually formed large glaciers that began to flow toward the equator.

Once the glaciers began forming, they created a feedback loop and increased the chilling effect on the climate. This was mostly due to the fact that ice and snow have a much higher albedo than rocks, soil, or vegetation. The higher albedo of the glaciers caused more sunlight to be reflected back into space. The more the glaciers grew, the colder it got. As we will soon discover, this type of feedback process can also have a warming effect on the climate.

As Earth cooled, the glaciers continued to advance until they wound up covering about one-third of the planet. This process did not happen quickly. It took thousands of years for the ice to build up. As Earth continued to move through its different orbital cycles, the factors that originally combined to cool the planet fell out of alignment. Things then began to warm up again, causing the glaciers to melt.

The Milankovitch theory doesn't provide all the answers when it comes to how and why the ice ages happened when they did. Even with these problems, however, the theory does show how even relatively small variations in temperature can have an enormous impact on the long-term climate patterns on Earth.

SHORT-TERM CLIMATE CHANGES

Not all climate change happens slowly. Although the changes brought about by the Pleistocene ice ages took place over thousands of years, there have been times when climate shifts have happened over a much shorter period of time. One example of this was the so-called "little ice age," which lasted from the early 1400s to around 1900. One reason that it is hard to pin down exact dates for this event is that, unlike the large-scale glacial periods of the Pleistocene Epoch, the effects of the "little ice age" didn't happen the same way at the same time all over the planet. This has led to a great deal of debate among scientists about what actually happened. In fact, they can't even agree whether it was a single event lasting a few hundred years, or many smaller events lasting a few decades each.

Here's what scientists do know: At the beginning of the fifteenth century, winter temperatures, which had been fairly mild, once again began to drop in Europe, Greenland, and North America. Unfortunately, because the first accurate weather thermometer wasn't perfected until 1714 by Gabriel Daniel Fahrenheit, there are no detailed temperature records for this time. Instead, scientists have had to rely on journals kept by people who wrote about the harsh, bitter conditions. Scientists also have been able to infer temperature information from several other **proxy** records, including tree rings, lake deposits, and ice and ocean sediment cores. Exactly how these proxy records work will be discussed in the next chapter.

Based on this data, it appears that for some reason the overall global temperature dropped by about 1.8°F (1°C). This small change had a big impact on the planet. Sea ice around Iceland and Greenland became so thick that the Norse settlers there were cut off from their supply ships. Mountain glaciers in such far-reaching places as the Alps, Lapland, Alaska, and even New Zealand began advancing again. Canals in Holland froze solid, and storms became so severe that many dikes were breached and thousands of people drowned.

One of the biggest problems in sorting out the data is that these climatic changes did not happen evenly. Over the 400- to 500-year span of the little ice age, temperatures fluctuated quite a bit. Even though the global temperature was generally cooler, there were also years that were unusually warm. Then, starting around 1850, the

What Triggered the Ice Ages?

Although the Milankovitch theory does a fairly good job of explaining the cyclic nature of the most recent ice ages, it does not explain what triggered the first Pleistocene glacial period to occur some 2 million years ago. For that, we

(continues)

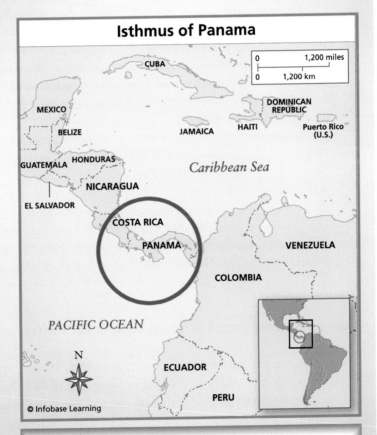

Isthmus of Panama

CUBA

MEXICO

BELIZE

GUATEMALA   HONDURAS

NICARAGUA

EL SALVADOR

COSTA RICA

PANAMA

JAMAICA   HAITI

DOMINICAN REPUBLIC

Puerto Rico (U.S.)

Caribbean Sea

VENEZUELA

COLOMBIA

PACIFIC OCEAN

N

ECUADOR

PERU

© Infobase Learning

0   1,200 miles

0   1,200 km

Figure 2.3   The Isthmus of Panama was formed 3 million years ago during the Pliocene epoch. Its formation caused the creation of the Gulf Stream current.

(continued)

have to leave the poles and head toward the equator to take a look at some plate tectonic action. If you look at a modern map of the world, you'll see that in-between the continents of North and South America, there is a narrow strip of land called the Isthmus of Panama. This is where the Panama Canal is located today. This land is the only thing keeping the Atlantic and Pacific oceans from joining each other.

According to global reconstructions, the Isthmus of Panama is actually a relatively recent land feature. Before the start of the Pleistocene epoch, reconstructions show that North and South America were separated by water. This meant that ocean water freely circulated around the globe near the equator, helping to distribute heat energy evenly around the planet.

When the isthmus closed, it changed the circulation pattern in the oceans. In the Atlantic Ocean, water now flowed from the poles to the equator. As the cold arctic water entered the system, it cooled the ocean. This in turn cooled the climate. Many geologists believe that this change in circulation is what triggered the first Pleistocene glacial period. After that, they believe the orbit changes kicked in to control the ebb and flow of the ice sheets.

overall cooling trend started to reverse itself. It has been rising ever since.

Scientists are not sure exactly what caused the little ice age, or if there was only one single cause. Some have speculated that increased volcanic activity in the fourteenth century put large amounts of dust into the atmosphere, which caused sunlight to be reflected back into space. Others have blamed it on the Sun itself. It turns out that from 1645 to 1715 (a period called the Maunder minimum), the Sun had very little sunspot activity. Sunspots are dark patches that can be seen on the surface of the Sun. They are believed to be magnetic storms. When sunspot activity is high, the overall energy output of the Sun increases. This, in turn, would cause Earth to warm.

During the Maunder minimum, there were almost no sunspots visible on the sun. This has led some scientists to conclude that the energy output of the Sun was less.

These days a growing number of scientists believe that much of the climatic change that happened in Europe and North America during the little ice age may be linked to changes in the circulation patterns of the atmosphere and a phenomenon called the North Atlantic Oscillation, or **NAO** for short. Unequal heating of the air by Earth's surface produces high and low pressure zones in the atmosphere. Under normal conditions there is a large low-pressure zone over the northern Atlantic Ocean called the Icelandic Low. South of this system is a high-pressure zone called the Azores High. Because of the Coriolis effect, the air above the Icelandic Low moves in a counter-clockwise direction and the air above the Azores High spins clockwise. The result of these two spinning systems is a flow of air from west to east across the Atlantic from North America toward Europe. The pressure differences and locations of these two zones are not constant. They tend to move back and forth over time. This movement is a major controlling factor of the climate of both eastern North America and Western Europe.

When there is a large pressure difference between the Icelandic Low and Azores High, the NAO is said to be in a positive phase. This results in very strong westerly winds that bring cool summers, but warmer and wetter winters over much of Europe and eastern North America. When the NAO is in a negative phase, the pressure difference between the Icelandic Low and Azores High is not as great. As a result, the westerly winds die down and arctic air flows down over Europe and North America, creating extremely cold winters. Based on recent studies, it appears that during the little ice age both phases of the NAO appeared to have been much more intense. This would have resulted in much colder winters with many more extreme storm events.

EL NIÑO: ONE BAD LITTLE BOY

In recent years, the media has been filled with stories about a sudden climatic change that often lasts only a few years at most.

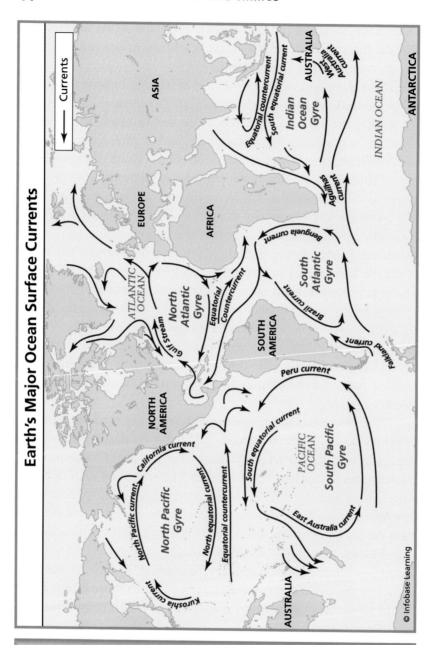

Figure 2.4 Surface water movement in the ocean takes place in the form of currents. Currents move ocean water horizontally at the surface. These surface currents are driven mainly by the wind and other forces, such as the Coriolis effect. The location of land masses affects surface current patterns, creating huge circular patterns called current gyres. From the equator to middle latitudes, the circular motion is clockwise in the Northern Hemisphere and counterclockwise in the Southern Hemisphere.

Usually this event is referred to simply as El Niño, which is Spanish for "boy" or "little boy." Its full name is the El Niño Southern Oscillation, or **ENSO**, for short. Like the North Atlantic Oscillation, El Niño is caused by a shift in atmospheric conditions, except instead of taking place over the Atlantic Ocean, it happens in the Pacific. Like the NAO, ENSO controls weather conditions over a wide geographic area. In recent years the effects of El Niño appear to have gotten stronger. Scientists believe that it has been responsible for a wide range of natural disasters.

El Niño was named by Peruvian fisherman. The name is a reference to Jesus Christ as an infant because its effects are usually felt in the coastal waters off Peru right around Christmas time, when Christians celebrate Christ's birth. To understand how it works, it is necessary to go back and take a look at how the Coriolis effect controls the flow of air and water in the Pacific Ocean.

The trade winds in the Pacific generally blow from east (the Americas) to west (Asia). This is because there is normally a large low-pressure zone over the western Pacific Ocean and a high-pressure zone in the east. As the winds blow across the ocean near the equator, they literally push the surface water along with them, creating two large gyres. The one north of the equator flows in a clockwise direction and the southern gyre flows counterclockwise. In between these two strong, westward-flowing currents is a weak countercurrent that flows eastward along the equator.

As the main currents flow westward across the ocean they pick up a tremendous amount of heat and deliver it to Asia. When the warm water arrives at the western side of the Pacific, it heats the air. This enhances the normal low-pressure zone that is found there. The warm, rising air currents are quite humid, and they eventually release their stored water as the annual monsoon rains upon which farmers in Asia depend.

As water flows across the ocean from east to west, along the coast of North and South America, new water flows from the poles toward the equator to fill the space. This polar water is quite cold, especially along the coast of South America where the Peru Current flows north from Antarctica. Not only is the Peru Current cold, but it is also rich in nutrients, creating an ideal habitat for plankton. These tiny organisms form the base of the food chain for a wide range of fish species, especially anchovies. This makes the region one of the most productive fisheries in the world.

Boys Can't Have All the Fun

In most cases, after an El Niño event ends, the trade winds return to normal. Sometimes, however, the trade winds become exceptionally strong. When this happens, cold water begins to come up from below and water starts to move into the central and eastern Pacific Ocean. Scientists call this cold water event following an El Niño event *La Niña*, which means "little girl."

An El Niña event creates a large high-pressure system over the ocean in the atmosphere south of Alaska. This helps redirect the jet stream farther north over Canada, bringing extremely cold winter weather to the central plains of the United States.

Toward the end of December, which is the start of summer in the Southern Hemisphere, the Peru Current will often shut down for a few weeks. The cold, nutrient-rich water gets replaced by a warm, nutrient-poor tropical current flowing south along the coast from the equatorial countercurrent. When this happens, the fish disappear and the local economy suffers. Most of the time, the warming trend only lasts a short time and the currents quickly return to their normal pattern.

Every few years, instead of returning to normal, the warming trend along the west coast of the Americas gets stronger, unleashing a major El Niño event. Over the last few centuries, large-scale El Niño events have happened every two to seven years. Over the last few decades, however, they appear to be stronger and more frequent. Scientists believe that major El Niño events happen because the normal atmospheric pressure zones over the Pacific Ocean break down and flip. In other words, air pressure begins to rise in the low-pressure zone in the western Pacific and falls in the high-pressure zone in the east. This pressure imbalance weakens the trade winds and the warm water that was stored in the western Pacific begins to flow back across the ocean. The eastward-flowing equatorial countercurrent becomes very strong and brings a large mass of warm water with it across the Pacific Ocean.

Scientists are not exactly sure what creates these pressure reversals. When El Niño is strong, it creates a major climate shift. Instead of monsoon rains there are extensive heat waves and droughts in Asia and Australia. The Pacific Northwest, which is normally wet, becomes dry while torrential rains fall on Southern California and Central America, creating floods and mudslides. In 1998, a particularly destructive El Niño is thought to have been responsible for more than $100 billion in damage.

One of the biggest questions that climate scientists are facing today is what effect global warming will have on phenomena such as El Niño and the NAO. Before they can answer this question, however, they must first answer an even bigger question: Is Earth really getting warmer?

The Evidence
For and Against
Global Warming

There are many stories in the media that debate whether global warming is a myth. Some people outright deny the existence of global warming, claiming that all the talk about it is really just part of a big conspiracy by scientists who want to make people scared so that they can get more government funding for their work. Others, such as former U.S. President George W. Bush, have said that there is no scientific proof that global warming is happening and that, rather than jump into things too quickly, the matter needs to be studied more.

The truth of the matter is that there is a great deal of hard data showing that Earth's surface temperature is getting warmer. Even though definite proof may still be missing, there is more than enough scientific evidence to reach the conclusion that global warming is for real and that it is already having an effect on the planet. What follows is a look at some of the evidence that global warming is indeed happening, and at some of its possible causes.

TAKING EARTH'S TEMPERATURE

One of the biggest challenges that scientists face when it comes to studies of global climate is having enough accurate data on which to base their analysis. To a casual observer this would seem to be fairly straightforward. The easiest way to find out if the global temperature is rising is to simply compare the current temperature to the temperature in the past.

There are a few problems with this direct approach. These days, scientists have many ways to measure Earth's temperature and plenty of data to use for analyses. There are literally thousands of weather stations both on land and at sea that make up a global network that continuously reads and records surface temperatures. In addition, orbiting satellites and weather balloons are used to regularly monitor the temperature of both the ocean and the atmosphere.

Many of these measurement techniques are fairly new. Wide-scale weather satellites didn't start flying until the 1970s, and the sophisticated computer networks used to collect and integrate all the surface data didn't start developing until a few years after that. In addition there were far fewer ground-based weather stations in the past, so the global coverage was nowhere near as good as it is today.

Even with these limitations, however, most climate scientists believe that they have enough direct temperature readings to show that, during the past century, Earth's average surface temperature has increased about 1.1%, or about 1.2°F (0.74°C). They show that the decade between 1999 and 2009 was the warmest 10-year period ever recorded.

Not all scientists are convinced that this data provides a totally accurate picture of what's happening on Earth. More than a few people have raised questions about the reliability of the temperature data.

First, they point out, temperature readings taken today at official weather stations are generally done using sophisticated digital probes that immediately log the data into a computer. Since the readings are taken automatically and are taken the same way each time, the data is very consistent and there is almost no room for human error. Less than 40 years ago, this was not the case. In the past, most temperature readings at weather stations were taken by people using old-fashioned, non-digital thermometers. In many cases, the temperature readings were taken at different time intervals by different people, and in some cases, readings were missed and errors were made in the weather logs.

Some scientists argue that the further back in time you look, the less reliable the temperature data becomes. They feel that trying to compare this past data to the current data is just bad science. Of course, many other scientists point out that even if these types of errors happened at a few locations, they would be relatively small when compared with the total number of accurate readings. The end result would be that the errors, if they do exist, would have only a small impact on the total analysis.

A second problem has to do with the location of some of the weather stations and how changes in local conditions over the years might have affected the temperature readings. Chapter 1 discussed the heat island effect, and showed how increasing the number of roads, buildings, and parking areas can cause the air around the paved areas to warm up several degrees. As it turns out, many of the long-term weather stations, especially in the United States and Europe, are located in areas that have seen significant amounts of development during the last 50 years.

Some scientists argue that the higher temperature readings that are being recorded at some of these stations today may not be giving an accurate measure of the true climate change. Instead, the readings may just be recording a local temperature increase brought about by more pavement and less open space. Other climate scientists are quick to point out that much of the global climate data being used today is based on sea surface temperatures, which is not impacted in any way by the heat island effect.

Since the 1990s there have been several temperature studies that have raised a few red flags when it comes to the idea that the planet is getting warmer. The first involved a study of the temperatures of the lower atmosphere. This study was conducted by John Christy, a climate scientist working at the University of Alabama in Huntsville. In 1992, he conducted an analysis of temperature data taken from both satellites and weather balloons. His findings clearly showed that the troposphere was cooling when compared to Earth's surface. If this were true, it would seriously damage the case for global warming, because if the surface is getting warmer, so should the lower atmosphere.

As it turns out, Christy's analysis wasn't wrong—the data was. After being confronted with this issue, other climate scientists went back and checked the data. They found that there were significant errors in the way the atmospheric temperatures were recorded. Corrections were published in 2005. When a new analysis was conducted, it showed that the troposphere was also warming, along with the planet's surface.

A second study that has been championed by global warming skeptics concerns temperature trends in Antarctica. Originally published by a group of climate researchers in the scientific journal *Nature,* the study concluded that the temperature of the eastern interior Antarctic continent actually declined between 1966 and 2000. This was immediately used by some in the media as "proof" that global warming was a hoax. The findings in this study were supported by another Antarctic climate study published in 2009. In this later study, the authors showed that the cooling was only impacting a small region of Antarctica. The entire continent taken as a whole, they reported, had actually warmed by 0.9°F (0.5°C) when measured during a 50-year period. It further showed that the cooling in eastern Antarctica was due to a shift in the wind pattern over the continent, which was keeping the heat from reaching the interior.

This last situation reinforces an important point: When scientists speak about global warming, they are talking about an increase in the average surface temperature of the entire planet. This means that different regions may experience different amounts of temperature increase. Some, such as eastern Antarctica, may even see a local cooling.

INDIRECT INDICATORS OF A CHANGING CLIMATE

Direct temperature readings aren't the only lines of evidence to suggest that the planet is heating up. There are a variety of indirect temperature indicators that also provide clues about what Earth's climate was in the past. One of the best indicators of what weather conditions were like in the past can be found in the historical records that people kept back then. Much of the information about the little ice age came from letters and journals that people kept during that time. Even though they can't be given the same scientific weight as direct weather measurements, historical records can offer many clues about the existence of early frosts, cold spells, droughts, and heat waves.

Written documents such as old newspapers and farmers' planting records, as well as diaries kept by travelers, contain a wealth of information about local weather conditions. Logbooks from ships are particularly useful because the captains and mates who kept them were often trained to make accurate observations about the conditions of the sea and sky. Many of these vessels covered a wide geographic area, providing historians and climate scientists with a snapshot of weather conditions for a particular month or season. Historical records coupled with other indirect measurements allow climate scientists to piece together a picture of how climates have changed over different regions.

GLACIERS AND ICE SHEETS

Glaciers are found on many of the mountains around the world. Mountain glaciers are like extremely slow-moving rivers of ice that flow down from the top of mountains into the valleys below. They can be found on every continent except Australia and can even exist in tropical regions if the mountain is tall enough. Both Mt. Kilimanjaro in Tanzania and Mt. Kenya have glaciers on their summits, even though they are located right near the equator.

Because it is so cold at these high altitudes, when snow falls it does not totally melt in the spring and summer. Instead, it gradually builds up in thickness. As it does, the snow at the bottom of the pile gets compacted and transformed into ice. During the course of many years the weight of new falling snow causes the ice to slowly flow downhill, forming a glacier.

As long as the snow continues to fall at the top of the mountain at the glacier's head, the glacier will continue to flow downhill, carrying rocks and soil with it. As the glacier moves down a valley, it eventually reaches a point where the temperature is above freezing. This causes the ice at the front of the glacier (called the *foot*) to melt. The length and volume of a glacier is controlled by the balance

Figure 3.1   Kilimanjaro glacier is seen from Uhuru peak in Tanzania in December 2010. Between 1912 and 1953, the mountain's ice cover shrank about 1% each year. From 1989 to 2007, that rate sped up to 2.5% a year, and the rate is increasing. Since 2000, the mountain's three remaining ice fields have shrunk by 26%.

between the amount of snow accumulating at the head and the rate at which the ice is melting at the foot.

How far a glacier travels down a valley depends on several factors. In order to keep flowing downhill, the glacier must keep getting new snow at its head. If the rate of snow decreases, or if the air temperature gets warmer, the ice will melt faster and the glacier will begin to retreat back up the valley. It is important to note that the glacier never moves backward. It always moves forward (downhill). If the rate of melting at the foot exceeds the rate of forward motion, however, the glacial front moves back up the valley. This is exactly what is happening today to mountain glaciers all over the world.

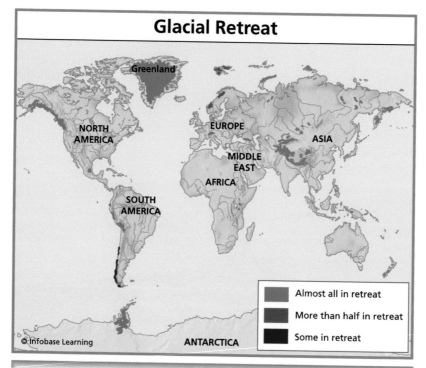

Figure 3.2 This map shows the locations of the world's melting glaciers. If global warming continues, some day these glaciers may be gone forever.

During the last century and a half, scientists who monitor the position and thickness of glaciers have noticed a significant trend, with ice loss in temperate and tropical regions being the worst. Since 1850, for example, mountain glaciers in the European Alps have lost as much as 40% of their surface area and about half their total volume. In New Zealand's Southern Alps, the surface area loss has been around 25%. On Mt. Kilimanjaro, it's been a whopping 60%. In polar regions, mountain glaciers have not been melting as quickly as in other parts of the world because the temperatures still stay below freezing most of the year. Even so, there has been a measurable loss, generally ranging from 2% to 6%.

Some scientists who do not support the idea of global warming point out that the fact that glaciers are retreating more in some areas

Figure 3.3 These images of Muir Glacier in Alaska's Glacier Bay National Park clearly show glacier melt. The upper black and white image was taken in 1899, when Muir Glacier filled Muir Inlet. By 2003, as the color image taken from a similar location shows, the glacier melted significantly and retreated approximately 30 miles (38 km).

than others could be the result of regional changes in temperature. This may not reflect a global change, they argue. In addition, they note that temperature is not the only factor that can cause a mountain glacier to retreat. If an area experiences a reduction in snowfall, there will be less snow accumulating at the head of a glacier, so the downhill flow will be reduced. Although this last fact is true for some areas, in other regions snowfall has stayed pretty constant and the glaciers are still retreating. In addition, at the present time there are almost no places in the world where glaciers are growing, suggesting that the impact is not just a regional change.

Mountain glaciers aren't the only forms of ice found on the planet that are currently experiencing an increase in the rate of melting. Because they get only small amounts of solar radiation, both the North Pole and the South Pole have a year-round cover of ice. At the South Pole is the continent of Antarctica, on top of which lies a layer of ice that is several miles thick. This southern polar ice cap extends off the edge of the continent, forming floating ice sheets that cover large areas of the seas surrounding Antarctica. There is no land at the North Pole, but there is a large mass of sea ice that floats on top of the Arctic Ocean. Near the North Pole is the large island of Greenland, which, like Antarctica, is covered by a thick ice sheet.

During the last several decades scientists have recorded a significant loss of ice volume on both the Greenland and Antarctic ice caps. At the North Pole they have observed that the seasonal sea ice forms later in the autumn and winter and melts earlier in the spring. Using a variety of measurement techniques, these same scientists have determined that the permanent layer of sea ice has become much thinner and has lost a significant amount of its volume. In a report issued in September 2010 called The Arctic Report Card, researchers said that the mass of sea ice in the arctic region for that year was the third lowest recorded during the last 30 years. In addition, Greenland experienced record high ice loss when a piece of the ice cap the size of Manhattan Island broke away.

Taken together, these developments strongly suggest that the temperature near the poles has warmed considerably in just a few decades. If it continues, large areas of both the Arctic and Antarctic oceans that were once covered with winter ice may soon be ice-free.

PROXY TEMPERATURE MEASUREMENTS

Even though direct temperature measurements on Earth only go back about two centuries, it does not mean that climate scientists are totally in the dark when it comes to getting a handle on what the surface temperature was hundreds or even thousands of years ago. To get the data they need, scientists use a *proxy* measurement. A *proxy* is something that stands in for something else and provides the same type of information. In climate science there are a number of different proxies that paleoclimatologists use to chart the temperatures of the past. They include ice cores, sediment cores, tree rings, corals, and fossil pollen.

Ice Cores

Ice cores are long tubes of ice that are carefully cut from land-based ice sheets such as those found on Antarctica and Greenland. When it snowed in the past, the tiny ice crystals trapped bubbles that contain samples of the atmosphere at the time it snowed. By carefully drilling deep into the ice, climate scientists can extract cores that contain air bubbles going back literally thousands of years. These air bubbles record the concentration of carbon dioxide and other greenhouse gases that were in the atmosphere in the past. In addition, the ice surrounding them contains oxygen atoms that are the key to figuring out what the temperature was at the time.

Oxygen is the gas in the air that we depend on when we breathe. It also combines with hydrogen to make water molecules. Oxygen atoms aren't all the same, though. Oxygen comes in several different forms called **isotopes.** The most common isotope of oxygen is called O_{16}. The number 16 comes from the mass of the atom. Oxygen also comes in two heavier isotopes known as O_{17} and O_{18}. Back in the 1960s, scientists discovered that they could calculate past temperatures by comparing the number of heavy oxygen atoms to the number of light oxygen atoms found in ancient ice.

Here's how it works: When the air temperature gets cold, water vapor condenses to form rain or snow. Because they are heavier, water molecules containing O_{18} atoms tend to condense first. If the temperature continues to drop, then the lighter water molecules containing O_{16} atoms condense. By comparing the relative number of O_{16} atoms to the number of O_{18} atoms in the ice, and using modern-day ice to figure out the ratio, climate scientists can get an accurate reading on what the temperatures were when the ice formed. Ice core data shows that the planet is currently experiencing some of the warmest temperatures of the past 100,000 years.

SEDIMENT CORES

Sediment cores are similar to ice cores except that, instead of being made of ice, they are long tubes of mud extracted from the bottom of oceans or lakes. In these environments, sediment particles slowly accumulate. This often provides scientists with a long and undisturbed record that goes back hundreds and even thousands of years. As with ice cores, the farther you go down the core from the top to the bottom, the farther back in time you are. Instead of looking for trapped air bubbles, sediment researchers look at the composition of the sediment and the shells of sea creatures that are buried in the mud.

With a sediment core taken from the North Atlantic Ocean, the first thing you see is alternating dark and light bands. Upon closer inspection, the dark layers are seen to be made up generally of coarse mineral grains (sand), while the lighter layers are composed of the shells of tiny creatures called foraminifera, or *forams* for short. These creatures have shells composed of calcium carbonate ($CaCO_3$), which, like ice, has the element oxygen in it.

Using similar techniques to those used on ice cores, chemists can work out the ratio of O_{16} to O_{18} atoms found in the shells. They can then calculate the temperature the water was when the creatures were alive. The concentration of O_{18} relative to O_{16} increases as the water gets colder. As with the ice cores, sediment cores from the ocean support the idea that there has been a steady increase in sea surface temperature during the past century.

Tiny sea creatures aren't the only things that scientists analyze in sediment cores. When inland lakes are studied, the main objective is to find fossilized pollen. In addition to making people sneeze and turning their eyes red, pollen is an excellent indicator of past climates. Each type of plant has its own uniquely shaped pollen grains, which can be used like a fingerprint to determine the genus or

Figure 3.4 Varves are layers of sediment that form annually, like the rings of a tree.

species of that plant. Most pollen grains are extremely durable, so when they get buried in sediment they are preserved very well.

The concept of studying pollen grains is pretty straightforward. Different plants live in different environments and in different climates. By matching the preserved pollen in the sediment core with the plant that it came from, scientists can get a really clear idea of what the climate was like for each layer of sediment in the core.

As climates change, the type of pollen found in the core will also change. In many lakes, sediment accumulates on the bottom in thin annual layers called varves. Under a microscope, varves can be counted, with each layer representing one year. By counting down from the top and identifying the pollen found at each layer, scientists can reconstruct the climate history for the region around the lake with a high degree of accuracy. Based on these studies, climatologists have shown that there has been a gradual shift of plant species from tropical regions to higher latitudes. This strongly suggests that the climates in these areas are indeed getting warmer.

TREE RINGS

Perhaps the most important climate proxy (and most controversial) is the use of **dendrochronology**, or tree ring dating. The main ideas

Corals Also Get Into the Act

While some climate scientists are drilling into the seafloor looking for temperature records hidden in the shells of microscopic organisms, others go right to the source. Corals are tiny animals that live in large colonies in shallow ocean environments. These animals attach themselves to a rock or other stationary object and secrete an exoskeleton made from calcium carbonate ($CaCO_3$). Over time, the skeletons of individual animals pile on top of each other, forming large structures called coral reefs.

As with forams, the elements used to make the skeletons come from the surrounding seawater. Under normal conditions, most corals secrete skeletons faster in the summer than in the winter, when the water is cooler. As a result, the coral skeletons usually show seasonal growth bands when viewed under a microscope. By drilling into a coral reef from the top down and counting backwards, scientists can get an accurate reading of when the corals formed.

Once scientists have established the year of growth, they then analyze the ratio of O_{16} to O_{18} atoms found in the coral skeletons. Next they calculate the temperature of the water in the same way they do forams.

There are still some glitches to be worked out before coral growth lines can be used as reliable climate indicators. Still, since corals have been building reefs around the world for a very long time, it is hoped that they will be able to provide climate scientists with a way to reconstruct sea surface temperatures for hundreds or even thousands of years.

behind the technique are similar to those used in studying corals. Every year that a tree is alive, it adds a new layer of wood to its trunk and branches. This growth does not happen evenly throughout the year. Usually a tree will grow faster during the spring when it is wet than in the summer months when it tends to be dry. As a result, the cells of the new wood that grow in the spring are larger than those that form later in the growing season. Growth pretty much stops in the winter when the tree is dormant, and then it picks up again the next spring.

If you were to bore into a tree trunk and remove a core, you would see this difference in growth as a series of rings. Each one would correspond to a different year, with the oldest ring in the center of the tree and the youngest on the outer edge, right below the bark. By counting the rings from the outside in, a specialist in dendrochronology can easily determine a tree's age. If the tree is still alive, he or she can tell the exact year that it started to grow.

Variations in tree ring growth don't just happen with the changing seasons. Scientists have found that a number of different climatic factors, including the amount of sunlight, the amount of rainfall, and the local temperature, can all affect how fast cell growth takes place. In general, the warmer and wetter a growing season is, the wider the tree ring will be for that year. By "reading" the rings in very old trees, climate scientists can estimate what the climate was like hundreds of years ago. Then, by overlapping the tree ring patterns found in living trees with those found in logs and stumps of dead trees, they can push the chronology back hundreds, and in some cases thousands of years.

Since trees are found all over the world, this approach would seem to be the answer to a climate scientist's dream. But there are some problems with the technique that have occasionally turned the dream into a nightmare.

One big problem with dendrochronology is that different species of trees respond to changing environmental conditions in different ways. You may have heard the expression "you can't mix apples and oranges." In the same way, you really shouldn't compare the growth data from a bristlecone pine tree with that of an oak. Because different trees are adapted to different environments, it is very difficult to find a single species of tree growing all over the world. This means that scientists are limited to comparing the growth data of only similar species in a relatively small region, not the entire globe.

Figure 3.5 The scientific method of figuring out the age of a tree based on its pattern of tree rings is called dendrochronology.

A second problem with tree rings is that individual trees show a great deal of variation in the way they grow. The environmental factors that affect their growth can change from tree to tree. Even though temperature and moisture are the two main things control-ling growth, other factors, including soil conditions, slope, and access to sunlight, can have a major impact on how fast tree rings form. This means that two trees of the same species on different sides of the same hill can have very different growth patterns. In order to get an accurate reading of a regional climatic change, it is necessary to sample literally hundreds of trees to compare their individual growth patterns. In many cases, the sample sizes that climate scientists are using are not really big enough to rule out the possibility that other conditions could have caused a change in growth patterns.

One final problem that has been raised by some scientists concerning tree ring data involves something called the *carbon dioxide fertilization effect*. During photosynthesis, all plants take in carbon dioxide from the atmosphere, which is where they get the carbon to make new cells. Carbon dioxide concentrations in the atmosphere have steadily increased during the last 150 years. The question is: Are trees showing an increased amount of growth because of warmer temperatures, or is it due to increased levels of carbon dioxide in the air?

If it is the carbon dioxide that's causing the extra growth, then scientists argue that tree ring data should not be used as a temperature proxy. The problem is further complicated by the fact that when attempts have been made to link tree growth patterns with actual temperature readings taken over the last century, they don't match up all that well. As a result, there are some serious questions about the reliability of tree ring data by itself when it comes to measuring temperatures of the past.

THE FINDINGS OF THE IPCC

As the number of scientists investigating different types of proxy data increased, the evidence that Earth's surface temperature was rising continued to mount. By the mid 1980s, political leaders began raising the issue of global warming at different international meetings. As a response to the growing concern, in 1988 the World Meteorological Organization (WMO) and the United Nations Environment Program (UNEP) set up the Intergovernmental Panel on Climate Change, or **IPCC** for short.

The main purpose of the IPCC is to provide governments of the world with a clear, unbiased, scientific view of what is happening to the world's climate, as well as the potential environmental and socioeconomic impacts that climate change might bring to different places on the planet. To accomplish this task, the IPCC draws on the expertise of thousands of different scientists from all over the world who work as volunteers to review the latest climate data and make recommendations. To ensure that all views are represented, participation in the IPCC is open to scientists from all the different member countries of the United Nations. It is important to note that the member scientists of the IPCC do not generally conduct original climate research themselves. Instead, they review the research conducted by other scientists and summarize the different findings in their reports.

In 1990, the IPCC released its first assessment report. It indicated that, based on the data available at that time, global warming was indeed happening. If global warming were ignored, the report continued, it would result in a large number of environmental as well as economic problems for many of the poorer countries in the world. Based largely on these findings, the member nations of the United Nations created the Framework Convention on Climate Change (UNFCCC). This was the first international treaty aimed at reducing global warming and dealing with the problems brought about by climate change. In 1995, the IPCC issued its second assessment report, which led to the adoption of the Kyoto Protocol of 1997.

The Kyoto Protocol, an international treaty, will be discussed later, but it is important to note that by 1997, most mainstream climate scientists recognized that global warming was indeed happening and that it posed a real threat to planet Earth.

THE HOCKEY STICK CONTROVERSY

During the late 1990s, the members of the IPCC weren't the only ones trying to figure out if global warming was a serious threat. Many independent climate scientists working at universities and research centers around the world were busy sorting through all the different temperature proxy data in an attempt to get a clear picture of what was really happening to Earth's climate.

One of the most important people doing this work was a climate scientist named Michael Mann. In 1999, Mann, along with his team at Penn State University, published a paper with a graph showing the average temperature in the Northern Hemisphere during the past thousand years. The graph showed only small variations in temperature for almost 900 years. Then, at the start of the twentieth century, there was a sudden and steep rise in temperature. The graph became known as the "hockey stick" graph because the shape of the plot resembled the bottom half of a hockey stick.

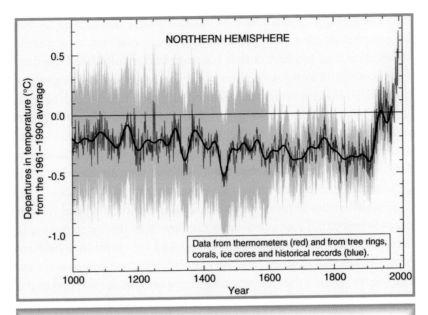

Figure 3.6 This graph, from the 1999 research paper "Northern Hemisphere Temperatures During the Past Millennium: Inferences, Uncertainties, and Limitations" by Michael Mann, Raymond S. Bradley, and Malcolm K. Hughes, was dubbed the "hockey stick graph" for its shape. It shows an abrupt rise in global temperatures in the late twentieth century after centuries of relative stability.

Climate scientists and other interested parties quickly took notice of the graph because it seemed to offer definitive proof that the surface temperature of the planet was rising. In addition, it showed that most of the temperature increase had occurred during a time when greenhouse gas emissions were also on the rise. This link suggested that human activities were a major part of the cause. The graph became a main focus of the book and movie *An Inconvenient Truth*, which popularized the idea that humans were to blame for global warming. It was also featured in the third assessment report of the IPCC, which was released in 2001.

At the time the graph was first published, most climate scientists were supportive of Mann's work and felt that he was on the right track. Several people, however, did raise questions about the way the data was processed and where Mann's team got it. Unfortunately, in the beginning, Mann and his colleagues were hesitant to release the supporting data so other scientists could evaluate it for themselves. This lead to charges that his team had manipulated the data so that it didn't accurately show what was really happening to the climate. To make matters worse, some private e-mails that had been written between Mann and other climate scientists were stolen and leaked onto the Internet. To a person not trained as a climate scientist, these e-mails seemed to suggest that he had somehow faked the data. The controversy mushroomed and was soon being referred to as "climate gate" on many popular news shows and Web sites.

Finally, at the request of the U.S. Congress, the National Academy of Sciences did a comprehensive review of all the current climate data, including the work done by Mann and his team. In a 2006 report, the academy agreed that the team's basic conclusions were indeed accurate, and that the warming trend seen in the last half of the twentieth century was greater than any other that had happened in the last thousand years. They further stated that the conclusion was supported by a wide range of evidence, including large-scale surface temperature reconstructions, as well as a variety of proxy indicators, such as the melting of ice caps and glaciers around the world.

At the suggestion of the academy report, Mann and his team have since conducted another temperature reconstruction going back two thousand years, based on additional proxy data. Although it does show more temperature ups and downs than the original "hockey stick" graph, the team's conclusion is the same. Not only is the world hotter now than it was during any other period in the last thousand years, but temperatures are also still on the rise. In 2007, the IPCC released its fourth assessment report on climate change, in which it was noted that 11 of the 12 warmest years on record (going back to 1850) happened between 1995 and 2006. The IPCC went on to state: "Warming of the climate system is unequivocal." In other words, in the minds of most of the world's leading climate scientists, global warming is real.

WHAT'S CAUSING GLOBAL WARMING?

Even though there are still a few individuals who claim that wide-scale global warming is not happening, the vast majority of climate scientists are in agreement that the planet is getting warmer. The big question is, are humans to blame or is most of the warming the result of natural climate variations? The answer to this question is critical because if humans are to blame, humans also might be able to take action to reverse the trend, much like what was done with the hole in the ozone layer in the latter part of the twentieth century. If the warming is due to natural causes, however, then there may be little, if anything, that humans may be able to do to cool the planet.

At this point in time, most climate scientists seem to be in agreement that humans have to accept at least some of the blame for the current warming trend. In 2004, Naomi Oreskes, a science historian working at the University of California, San Diego, published a report in the journal *Science* in which she reviewed 928 scientific papers dealing with climate change. She found that none of the studies disagreed with the idea that humans had some role in the current warming trend. Then, in January 2009, a poll conducted with more than three thousand earth scientists found that 82% believed that human activity is a significant contributing factor to changing Earth's average temperature. Clearly, there is a consensus among scientists that humans are impacting the global climate. But how?

The main input into Earth's energy balance is solar radiation. Some supporters of the idea that global warming is caused by natural forces have raised questions concerning fluctuations in the amount of radiation generated by the Sun. They point out that even a small increase in solar radiation would have a significant warming effect on Earth.

During its 11-year sunspot cycle, the amount of energy coming from the Sun does fluctuate. The Sun appears to have a slightly higher energy output during periods of high sunspot activity, and then it drops slightly when sunspot activity is low. Low sunspot activity is thought to be one of the contributing factors that brought on the little ice age. Since 1978, solar scientists have been able to directly measure the Sun's energy output, and they have confirmed these energy fluctuations. They also have found that the fluctuations happen in a small range, and that there has been no measurable upward or downward trend in energy output during the more than three decades since 1978.

The one thing that stands out in the energy balance is the steady increase in the concentration of greenhouse gases in the

Spots on the Sun

People have known about sunspots since Galileo's time, yet there are still many questions concerning why they happen and what effect they have on Earth. Over the years scientists have observed that the 11-year sunspot cycle has many fluctuations in terms of the total number of sunspots that happen during maximum years. The truth is, during the last few years, sunspot activity has been extremely low.

Those individuals who blame sunspots for global warming therefore need to find another theory. If sunspots are the main cause of climate change, Earth's temperature should be declining rather than increasing. This would seem to rule out sunspots as being the main factor controlling the recent warming. What's scary is that scientists aren't sure what will happen to Earth's temperature the next time sunspots peak.

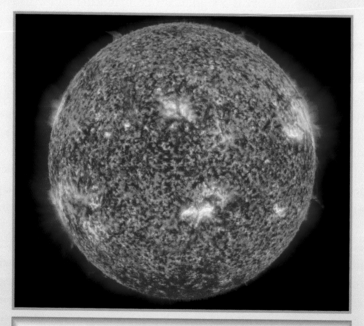

Figure 3.7   This high-definition image of the Sun was captured by NASA's Solar Dynamics Observatory in July 2010. Sunspot 1087 is on the upper right, while sunspot 1089 is in the lower left corner in this image.

atmosphere. Most of that can be pinned directly on humans. This was a major conclusion of the 2007 IPCC assessment report. The summary states: "Most of the observed increase in global average temperature since the mid-twentieth century is very likely due to the observed increase in **anthropogenic** greenhouse gas concentrations." *Anthropogenic* means "made by humans." When the report uses the term *very likely*, it means that statistically there is a more than a 90% chance that this is true.

The reason that the IPCC scientists can make this claim with such certainty is because the data on greenhouse gases is clear. In the report the panel makes the following observations about carbon dioxide and methane: As of 2005, the concentration of carbon dioxide gas in the atmosphere is 379 parts per million (ppm). During the last 650,000 years, the natural range of CO_2 has only varied between 180 and 300 ppm. This current value far exceeds anything in the natural range. When it comes to methane, things get even worse. During the same time period, natural concentrations of methane have varied between 320 and 790 parts per billion (ppb). According to the latest findings, the concentration of methane currently stands at a whopping 1,774 ppb.

What are the sources of all the extra greenhouse gases? The two most likely ones are land use changes and the burning of fossil fuels.

The amount of carbon dioxide and methane in the air is balanced by the carbon stored in living things. During the last 30 years, human development and the need for food has led to the widespread destruction of many of the world's forests. Not only do trees help remove carbon dioxide from the air, but when they are alive, they also store huge amounts of carbon in their wood. When forests are cleared for agricultural purposes, those trees that are not harvested for wood are usually burned, as is the underlying brush. This releases a tremendous amount of extra carbon dioxide into the air. Although it is true that the crops and grasses that replace the forests do take in some carbon dioxide when they grow, they don't produce wood and therefore don't store carbon.

By far, the biggest increase in greenhouse gases can be traced to the burning of fossil fuels, such as coal, petroleum products, and natural gas. Almost all of this activity can be traced back to the start of the industrial revolution in the late 1700s. At this time there was a major change in manufacturing. Instead of using water wheels or

Figure 3.8   Deforestation caused by the slash and burn technique of clearing land caused this destruction in Papua New Guinea.

windmills as a power source, factories began using steam engines, the most efficient of which were developed by James Watt. These steam engines burned wood and coal.

In the early 1800s, these same engines went mobile, making their way onto steam ships and railroad trains. These began replacing sailing vessels and coaches driven by horses. In the late 1800s, entrepreneurs including Thomas Edison and George Westinghouse began building coal-burning plants to generate electricity to power newly invented lights and other electrical appliances. Then, in 1885, Carl Benz built the first practical motorcar using an internal combustion engine. Many of these early automobiles were first fueled by alcohol, but when large reserves of cheap oil were discovered, they were quickly switched over to run on petroleum products. The final blow came in 1903 when the Wright Brothers placed an internal combustion engine in a glider, and the first fossil fuel-powered airplanes took to the skies.

Still, the fact that humans are burning fossil fuels, and the fact that fossil fuels release greenhouse gases does not prove that humans are to blame for the increase in greenhouse gases in the atmosphere. There are still, of course, natural sources of carbon dioxide and methane. Some of these sources include rotting organic material, animal respiration, and volcanic eruptions.

There is, however, one clue that suggests that fossil fuel burning may be to blame for the recent increase. When fossil fuels are burned, they release carbon that has been stored underground for literally millions of years. Carbon, like oxygen, has several different isotopes. Most of the carbon found in fossil fuels is called carbon 12 (C_{12}). There are also two heavier isotopes called C_{13} and C_{14}. Studies of the ratio of these isotopes in the atmosphere during the past several years shows that the ratio of C_{13} to C_{12} is getting smaller. This means that most of the carbon getting into the air is C_{12}, which is most likely coming from fossil fuels.

In recent years, the demand for energy has steadily increased, and so has the use of fossil fuels. Many industrialized countries including the United States continue to burn fossil fuels as the primary energy source. The problem is made worse by the fact that people in countries such as India and China, who have not had the same standard of living as those people in industrialized nations, now are demanding the same products and conveniences. As the millions of people in these countries start using more appliances and driving more cars, the amount of greenhouse gases that they release will sky-rocket. This idea is supported by the fact that in 2010 China passed the United States as the world leader in greenhouse gas emissions.

Unfortunately, the price of all this progress is not cheap. If humans continue on this trend, there will be some severe consequences.

How Will
Global Warming
Affect the Planet?

To say that global warming will affect the planet is really an inaccurate statement, because there is plenty of evidence to suggest that it is already having a major impact in certain regions of the world. The previous chapter discussed how rising temperatures are causing mountain glaciers to retreat and sea ice to thin. Global warming also appears to be having an impact on atmospheric circulation patterns, such as El Niño and the NAO. In its 2007 assessment report, the IPCC identified a number of areas where rising temperatures will have a direct impact on Earth's physical environment. What follows are some of the changes that are expected in the different regions of the world.

THE BIG THAW

Retreating glaciers and thinning sea ice are two lines of evidence to support the fact that the world is warming. As temperatures increase, this trend will continue, so much so that many of the world's mountain glaciers will actually disappear. In addition, the ice caps on Greenland and Antarctica are melting. The problem is no one is quite sure how fast this is happening.

One of the reasons that it is so difficult to know the speed of the melting is that both the Greenland and Antarctic ice sheets extend into the surrounding ocean, creating ice shelves. When an ice shelf breaks apart, it speeds up the rate at which the ice sheet behind it melts. In addition, the melting during the summer months causes lakes to form on top of the ice sheets. This water will often seep into the ice, making it melt faster.

Ice isn't the only thing that is melting in polar regions. In areas such as Alaska, Northern Europe, and Siberia large areas of the land surface are covered with permafrost. Permafrost is soil that is permanently frozen, so that even in summer it is rock hard below the surface. As the Earth warms, the permafrost melts. This creates many engineering problems for the local communities, because roads and buildings collapse as the ground underneath them thaws. Not only that, but permafrost also contains large amounts of methane trapped between the ice crystals.

Methane, like carbon dioxide, is a greenhouse gas. In fact, it is more than 20 times more effective than CO_2 at trapping heat. When this methane is released into the air, it can trap more heat, which will speed up the rate of warming. This type of process is called a *feedback loop,* and it's one of the unknown factors that climate scientists are trying to account for in their global warming predictions.

RISING SEAS

As mountain glaciers and ice sheets melt, they release a great deal of stored water, which eventually reaches the ocean. This causes sea levels to rise. During the past half-century, scientists working in coastal areas in many regions around the world have recorded just this type of increase. Based on these observations, scientists calculate that between 1961 and 2003 the average rate of worldwide sea level rise was 0.07 inches (1.8 mm) per year. What's even more disturbing is that the rate of rise between 1993 and 2003 was 0.12 inches (3.1 mm) per year. This shows that the rate of sea level rise is accelerating.

Melting ice is only one part of the reason that sea levels are rising. An even bigger contribution comes from something called **thermal expansion**. Air expands when it is heated. This same process happens in liquids, which explains how a liquid-filled thermometer works. In a way, the world's oceans behave just like a giant thermometer. Scientists estimate that since 1961, the oceans have been absorbing about 80% of the increased heat energy caused by global warming. As a result, average ocean temperatures have increased from the surface down to a depth of 9,800 feet (3,000 m). As ocean temperatures increase, the volume of the water also increases. The end result is a rise in global sea levels. For islands and low-lying coastal areas, even a rise of a couple of inches can spell disaster.

With rising seas comes the threat of increased flooding, especially from storm surges caused by severe storms and hurricanes. Land areas that were once out of flood zones will become inundated with water on a regular basis. This will lead to more coastal erosion, making it even more likely that roads, buildings, and other structures will be destroyed during storm events.

CHANGES IN OCEAN WATER

Not only is global warming changing the level of the sea, but it's also changing the physical properties of the water itself. Many species of marine animals are extremely sensitive to temperature changes. During the last 20 years, marine biologists have noted that large sections of coral reefs have been dying off due to a process called *bleaching*. Under normal circumstances, corals live in a symbiotic relationship with a type of algae, meaning that the organisms need each other to survive. If the water gets too warm, it disrupts the relationship between the corals and the algae. If it happens too often, the corals die. Over time corals may be able to adapt to the warmer ocean temperatures, but that's only if the warming happens at a slow rate.

All the extra carbon dioxide in the atmosphere isn't just changing the temperature of the ocean. It's having an effect on the chemistry of the seawater, too. Scientists estimate that between one-third and one-half of the extra CO_2 finds its way into the ocean. When carbon dioxide dissolves in water, it forms carbonic acid. Acidic solutions tend to react with and dissolve calcium carbonate ($CaCO_3$), which is what makes up most seashells and coral skeletons. During the last century, it is estimated that the average pH of the ocean has gone from 8.3 to 8.1. On the pH scale, the lower the number, the more acidic a solution. Although this may not seem like much of a change, many biologists believe that it has had an impact on the ability of marine invertebrates to make shells. As the ocean becomes more acidic, the problem will only get worse.

Another way in which global warming is changing the chemistry of seawater is by decreasing the amount of salt (salinity) it contains. As new fresh water enters the ocean from melting ice, it helps dilute the salt. One of the main forces driving the currents in the ocean is density. The differences in the density of polar and tropical water help to move the currents along. As ocean water becomes warmer and less salty, the density differences become narrower.

Many climate scientists are deeply concerned that if this trend continues, some major ocean currents, such as the Gulf Stream, might even shut down. Since ocean currents help distribute heat energy around the planet and play a major role in maintaining regional climates, this type of change could have tremendous impact on the weather patterns around the globe.

CHANGES IN WEATHER PATTERNS

A person doesn't need to be a climate scientist to recognize the fact that different parts of the world have been experiencing some wild weather in recent years: Record-breaking heat waves in Europe, record-breaking snowstorms in Washington, D.C., record-breaking rainstorms bringing floods to Pakistan, tornadoes hitting New York City, and Hurricane Katrina devastating the Gulf Coast in 2005.

None of these occurrences can be directly blamed on global warming. Taken together, however, these extreme weather events suggest that something strange is happening in the lower atmosphere. To a climate scientist, extreme weather is just what would be expected as the surface of the planet warms.

The reason has to do with some simple physics. Earth's surface heats the air above it, which in turn controls local and regional circulation patterns and weather conditions. Warmer ground and water temperatures mean that the air above the surface will heat and expand more quickly. This produces localized low-pressure zones, which in turn trigger high winds. Since warm air also has the ability to evaporate more water from Earth's surface, the relative humidity of the air also increases. Put low pressure together with high humidity and big temperature changes, and it's the perfect recipe for a thunderstorm.

Over the ocean in the tropics, things get even more intense. Hurricanes and typhoons get most of their energy from warm ocean water. As the warm air removes moisture from the ocean, the condensation of water vapor higher in the atmosphere releases what is called *latent heat* in the clouds. This sets off a cycle that results in the development of a tropical storm. If the storm keeps circulating over warm water, it intensifies and eventually becomes a hurricane in the Atlantic Ocean or a typhoon in the Pacific Ocean.

Although global warming has not been responsible for increasing the number of tropical storms, climate scientists believe that it has caused a significant increase in the intensity of these storms. Larger, more powerful hurricanes and typhoons will result in more damaging winds and storm surges. This means that there will be even more destruction and flooding to coastal areas when these storms hit.

Increased levels of evaporation and precipitation aren't limited to coastal areas. During normal years between July and September, a shift in the winds over the Indian Ocean brings warm, moist air toward India and Pakistan. When this air meets the cooler air over the continent, it begins to rain and continues to do so for several weeks. This annual event is called the *monsoon* and it's critical for supplying the region with water for agriculture and other uses.

In summer 2010, however, the rains that came were so severe that Pakistan experienced the worst flooding it has had in more than 80 years. By the time it was over, 62,000 square miles (160,580 km)—a land area roughly the size of England—was flooded and an estimated 1,600 people were killed. This is exactly the type of event that many climate scientists have predicted will happen as global temperatures rise.

While some areas may see more intense rainstorms during the warmer months, people living in the middle to higher latitudes may see more record-breaking snowstorms in the winter. One of the

Figure 4.1 Pakistani residents cling to each other as they walk through waters in the flood-hit Bakhtiyarabad area in the District of Sibbi on July 23, 2010. The 2010 Pakistan floods, which began in July of that year, left one-fifth of the country's land area under water. Pakistani officials said the heavier-than-usual monsoon rain, attributed to La Niña, caused almost 1,600 deaths and damaged or destroyed the property of about 20 million people.

biggest misconceptions that people have about global warming is the idea that it will snow less. Although it is true that some areas will experience less snow, others will see far more snow.

Here's why: In order for it to snow the air has to be humid and temperatures in the troposphere must be below the freezing point of water. Warmer air holds more water vapor than cold air. If the air is too cold, the humidity is so low that the water vapor present can't condense to form snow crystals. In areas where the air temperature is well below freezing, such as in Antarctica, there is very little snow.

If you take that same area and increase the temperature so that it is only slightly below freezing, the air is still cold enough to make snow, but it's warm enough to have a lot more water vapor.

In the winter of 2008, members of the U.S. Congress spoke out against the idea of global warming. They openly mocked former vice president Al Gore and other defenders of global warming by building igloos and snowmen on the Capital lawn during record snowstorms in Washington, D.C. If they had understood the science behind global warming a little more, they would have realized that what they were experiencing was exactly what climate scientists had predicted would happen as Earth's surface warmed.

Global warming will not bring increases in storm events all over the planet. When weather patterns change, it also means that some areas will see fewer storms. Fewer rain and snow events mean that in certain regions the climate is going to get really dry. Over the last decade there have been several stories of droughts hitting areas of the world that normally have abundant precipitation. One of these places is the Amazon rainforest.

By definition, a rainforest is a place that generally gets more than 160 inches (406 cm) of rain each year. This does not mean that it rains evenly throughout the year, though. Even in a rainforest there are wet seasons and dry seasons. Most of the Amazon River basin is located in Brazil, where the dry season takes place in the winter months, generally from May to October. Normally during the dry season the trees themselves help contribute rain to the system by pulling water out of the ground through their roots and then releasing it into the surrounding air. This process is called **transpiration**. Because of this natural water recycling, even during the dry season there is normally some rain.

During the dry season of 2010, however, things got really dry. Some of the smaller tributaries of the Amazon River dried up and the Negro River dropped to its lowest level since people began keeping records back in 1902. The drought lasted right through November and was called the drought of the century. The problem is that five years earlier, the Amazon Basin had experienced a similar drought that at the time was considered to be a freak occurrence. It also had been considered the drought of the century. In theory, only one of these events should happen once every hundred years or so, not twice in five years. In the 2005 drought, millions of trees died, releasing large amounts of carbon dioxide gas into the air. Under these

Big Winds in the Big Apple

When you think about tornadoes, the first place that comes to mind would probably be somewhere in the central portion of the United States, such as Kansas, Oklahoma, Nebraska, and Texas. This area, often called "tornado alley," is famous for the large number and intensity of the tornadoes that hit the region each year.

During the last few years, there have been a growing number of tornadoes in states such as Georgia, North Carolina, and Virginia—outside of this traditional belt. The real surprise came in 2010, when tornadoes hit New York City, a place where most meteorologists would never expect to see one. The weather conditions in New York City are normally such that it is almost impossible for tornadoes to form. Yet in 2010, the city was hit not once, but twice.

conditions, instead of being a "carbon sink," the forest was actually a net contributor of greenhouse gases.

CHANGES IN LIVING THINGS

Global warming can have tremendous impacts on different ecosystems in the world. All living things, from the simplest bacteria to polar bears, have certain adaptations that allow them to live in certain environments. When conditions in those environments change, they can either adapt to the new conditions, move somewhere else where the conditions are right, or else die.

In the case of corals, which are attached to the sea floor, moving is really not an option. As a result, many are simply dying in place. Other animals, such as humans, have the ability to adapt. Many other organisms are simply moving to new areas. Of course, even those who make the trip often find it tough going. As a result, some scientists predict that as many as a million species of plants and animals may be threatened with extinction if the current rates of habitat destruction and global warming continue.

Unfortunately, not all living things will be negatively impacted by global warming. As temperatures increase, many of the organisms that transmit infectious diseases will get a big boost. As a result, the diseases they carry will also spread. Take malaria, for instance. This disease is generally found in tropical regions and is carried by a particular type of mosquito that likes warm temperatures. As temperatures increase, so will the range of these mosquitoes. Consequently, new populations of people will be at risk of infection.

The other problem with infectious diseases concerns contaminated water supplies. When droughts happen, water becomes in short supply and the water that remains often gets tainted with disease-carrying organisms. This can also happen as the result of flooding, when water carrying sewage and other pollutants gets mixed with drinking water supplies. In either case, diseases such as cholera run unchecked, with the potential to sicken large portions of the population.

SOCIAL IMPACTS OF CLIMATE CHANGE

The physical changes brought about by climate change are bad, but from a human standpoint, the more important question is how these changes will impact our lives. Warmer temperatures mean rising seas, more severe storms, droughts, floods, and the spread of disease. All of these issues will impact society and test the abilities of both individuals and governments.

As with the physical impacts of global warming, social impacts will not affect all areas of the planet equally. People in developing countries will face far greater challenges than those in wealthier nations. Wealth alone, however, will not protect people from all of the problems brought about by climate change. What follows are a few of the more pressing issues that humans will face.

People on the Move

One place that is already feeling the direct effects of global warming is the Pacific island nation of Tuvalu. Located about halfway between Hawaii and Australia, Tuvalu is home to about 11,000 people, most of whom make their living from the sea. As a result of rising sea levels, the amount of land on the island has been steadily

A Rainforest Without the Rain?

It would be a huge understatement to say that scientists are concerned with what is happening to the climate of the Amazon Basin. Their biggest fear is that trees dying as a result of the 2010 drought will create a negative feedback loop that will cause the ecosystem to come crashing down: As more trees die, there will be fewer trees to recycle moisture. This would create a cycle of droughts that would stress the rest of the living trees to the point where the trees would not be able to survive. Rainforest regions would gradually change into grasslands similar to the savannah in Africa. At the present rate, many biologists believe that this all might take place before the end of this century.

If droughts in the rainforest become a regular occurrence, it will also set up the potential for more wildfires. This was the case after the drought of 2005 when thousands of fires released additional CO_2 into the air. The bottom line is that a cycle of droughts in the Amazon would have a major negative impact on Earth's climate. The Amazon has long been considered the "lungs" of the planet, taking CO_2 out of the air and storing carbon in trees. If this process reverses itself, there is no telling what the global consequences will be.

disappearing, threatening homes and businesses. The situation has gotten so bad that, in 2002, the government began relocating residents to New Zealand. If this trend continues, it's only a matter of time before the entire country, as well as its culture, disappears beneath the waves.

The residents of Tuvalu are an example of a growing class of people known as *environmental refugees*. These are people who must leave their homelands and move somewhere else because of severe environmental change such as droughts or floods. If you look at a map of the world showing population patterns, you'll see that the most densely populated regions of the world are found along the coasts. There are literally millions of people at risk from flooding due to rising sea levels. Where will they all go?

During the recent flooding in Pakistan, an estimated 20 million people were impacted. In many cases the neighbors of countries experiencing disaster do not have the resources to provide for their own people. Therefore taking in millions of new residents is out of the question. One of the most difficult things for people to do is share their resources with others, especially if it means giving up some of the things that they worked hard to get.

Famine

As climate patterns shift, so will a region's ability to produce food. Even though global warming may open up new agricultural areas closer to the poles, it will also have negative impacts on some of the places where food is currently being produced. Many countries of the world are already facing severe shortages of clean water and food. As the global population grows, the demand for food will increase. If just a few of the prime agricultural areas are lost to drought or heat waves, then the resulting food crisis will be a big one. Again, survival will come down to a willingness to share resources.

Governments in Chaos

As food, water, and energy resources get scarcer, people will be less likely to behave in a civil manner. From the Maya in Central America to the first settlers of Greenland, history is full of stories about past civilizations that have collapsed when the environment around them changed and food and water were in short supply. In some cases, dictators took over governments. In other cases, countries went to war with each other in the name of protecting their resources. The media is full of stories about the pending doom that will come about because of the effects of global warming.

Perhaps they are correct, but there is one important point that cannot be overlooked: We still have a choice in how the story is going to end. We can continue along the same path or we can decide to take action.

5

What Can Be Done To Address Climate Change?

Good news: Something can be done about global warming. Despite the fact that there are still climate deniers who claim that global warming is all a hoax and nothing needs to be done about it, a growing number of governments, scientists, and ordinary people are taking the issue seriously. They believe that some sort of action needs to be taken, and soon.

As with any problem, the first step in solving it is recognizing that there is a problem in the first place. Once the problem has been identified, then different solutions can be tried. This was the case when the Antarctic ozone hole was first discovered in the latter part of the twentieth century. Within a relatively short period of time, nations came together and an effective solution was found.

Unfortunately, the problems with global warming are far more complex, so the solutions are not going to be as easy or cheap. For argument's sake, let's agree with most climate scientists. We'll assume that the main cause of global warming is the increase in greenhouse gas concentrations in the atmosphere brought about by land use changes (primarily deforestation) and the burning of fossil fuels. If these are indeed the causes, then the solution should be simple:

All we would have to do is stop cutting down trees and stop using fossil fuels.

The problem is that if we were to do this, the entire world's economy would come to a crashing halt. Way too many things are tied to the use of fossil fuels to simply cut them out. In addition, people aren't cutting down forests because they hate trees. In most cases, the trees or the land that they occupy is the primary means of support for the people doing the cutting. In order to accomplish these goals, sudden change is out of the question. We need to ease into it. That's what the Kyoto Protocol was originally designed to do.

CHANGING ENERGY USE PATTERNS

Even without an international agreement, there are a great many things that nations and individuals can do to help reduce their **carbon footprint**. The trick is finding a way to reduce the use of fossil fuels while still having enough energy resources to meet peoples' needs.

The first and easiest step begins with conservation. Cutting down on energy waste will result in cuts in the amount of fossil fuels that are used. Many acts of conservation are really quite easy to do. It could be something simple, such as turning off unused lights and appliances, turning down the heat or air conditioner, or taking mass transit instead of driving. Other actions are a bit more costly in the beginning, but save money down the road. These include installing new windows and better insulation in buildings, trading in a gas-powered vehicle for a hybrid one, and replacing old heating and cooling systems with more efficient ones. By reducing waste, people can still do everything that they are used to doing, but they can do it without expending as much energy.

Yet simply cutting waste won't solve the problem by itself. Energy conservation can help cut some greenhouse emissions, but people still need to use a lot of energy. There are three main areas in which fossil fuels are used as the primary source of power. They are transportation, heating and cooling for industrial and residential uses, and electrical generation. In order to cut greenhouse emissions, each one of these areas has to start reducing the amount of fossil fuels being used. This can be done by switching to some other power

The Kyoto Protocol

The Kyoto Protocol is an international agreement that was adopted on December 11, 1997, in Kyoto, Japan. It came into force on February 16, 2005. The treaty is a legally binding agreement under which industrialized countries must reduce their emissions of greenhouse gases by about 5% compared to their emissions in the year 1990. The goal is to lower overall emissions of six greenhouse gases over a five-year period from 2008 to 2012.

In an attempt to be fair, the protocol recognized the fact that industrialized countries such as the United States and Japan were more responsible than developing countries for the high levels of greenhouse gases in the atmosphere. As a result, industrialized countries must make bigger cuts in emissions. National reduction targets ranged from 8% for members of the European Union and 7% for the United States, to 0% for Russia. Australia and Iceland were actually permitted to increase their emissions within certain limits.

source. Alternative energy technologies come into play here. There is a growing list of technologies that can be used to supply heat and generate electricity without having to burn fossil fuels. Let's take a look at electrical generation first.

GENERATING ELECTRICITY

Even though electrical power has only been available for a little more than a century, its use has steadily increased. Today it is the world's most versatile and important source of energy. Just stop and think of all the devices that you use on a daily basis that run on electricity. Where you would be without them?

As of 2007, the world was using a little less than 19 trillion kilowatt hours of electrical power each year. Of this, 67%, or roughly

Soon after the protocol was adopted it ran into problems, the biggest of which was the fact that the United States, at the time the largest emitter of greenhouse gases in the world, refused to ratify it. (It had still not done so as of April 2011.) There were a few reasons the U.S. government cited for not taking action. The most important was the fact that the protocol set no limits on the amount of greenhouse gases that developing nations such as China and India could release. Members of the U.S. government felt that this would pose a severe economic hardship on its own people while developing countries would be free to pollute as much as they wanted. In the end, 191 countries and the European Union did sign and ratify the agreement, which forms the backbone of an annual climate summit meeting.

Unfortunately, since signing the protocol, none of the member nations have been able to meet their target emission reductions. At best, some of them have been able to slow the rate at which they have increased the amount of greenhouse gases they are releasing. The treaty is set to expire in 2012, but there is hope that a new type of agreement can be reached in the future.

two-thirds, was generated from the burning of fossil fuels, 14% came from nuclear power, and about 18% came from **hydroelectric** power. Less than 1% came from renewable sources such as wind and solar energy. In order to make a serious dent in greenhouse gases, there has to be a major shift away from using fossil fuels to generate electricity.

These days many politicians and scientists are calling for a renewed push for nuclear power. Nuclear fission technology has been used for about 50 years and it releases almost no greenhouse gases. In this process, radioactive material is used to make steam, which turns a generator. It is effective, but it's just a really high-tech way to boil water. Accidents at nuclear power plants can release radioactive material into the air and water causing a whole host of environmental problems. Another drawback is that after it is used in a reactor to generate power, nuclear waste stays radioactive for

Figure 5.1 Steel drums containing nuclear waste are stacked at the Area 5 Radioactive Waste Management Site at Frenchman Flat in Nevada. The drums contain solid waste, made up of transuranics, which are radioactive chemical elements with heavy atomic nuclei that are made in nuclear reactions. These drums will be packed, 50 at a time, into steel cargo containers for storage above ground. Corrosion of these containers will be minimized because of the dry desert climate of the site.

thousands of years. Because of problems with finding a safe place to dispose of the waste products, and with the potential danger of an accident, the use of nuclear power in the United States has been limited.

People who are pushing for greater use of nuclear power point out that in France and several other European countries, the use of nuclear power is widespread and there have been very few accidents. They also point out that recent improvements in reactor safety mean that there is only a slim chance of having a nuclear disaster like the one that happened at the Chernobyl nuclear power plant in the Ukraine in 1986. But nuclear disasters can happen even in well-designed power plants. This became clear following the earthquake and tsunami that hit Japan in 2011, which damaged several nuclear reactors. The one thing that science hasn't come up with is a safe way to dispose of nuclear waste. At the present time, it is just being stockpiled until a permanent solution can be found.

For more than a century, hydroelectric plants have been using the power of water to create electricity. Historically, most of these installations have been quite large and extremely expensive. In addition, in order to build them, large dams must be constructed, creating huge natural lakes. This has a major impact on local communities and ecosystems. Several new developments are allowing utility companies to use small-scale hydro systems. These require

Figure 5.2 The Dalles Dam spans the Columbia River in Oregon. The Army Corps of Engineers began work on the hydroelectric dam in 1952 and completed it five years later.

Figure 5.3 Clusters of wind generators form multi-megawatt wind farms in Central California.

far lower construction costs and have smaller environmental impacts, so the use of this renewable power source should increase.

For the past 30 years or so, many European countries have been augmenting their fossil fuel-burning generators with **wind turbines**. These so-called wind farms have been proven reliable and have a fraction of the environmental impact of large-scale hydro systems. These systems are slowly making their way into the United States, but in many cases people are fighting their construction because they claim the wind turbines have negative environmental impacts. Most of these claims have been proven wrong. The only valid complaint is that they change the view of the landscape. Given a choice between watching a wind turbine spin and dealing with the effects of global warming, the decision would seem to be a simple one.

Of course, one of the best ways to obtain energy without having to use fossil fuels is to go right to the source: the Sun. Over the past decade there have been many new developments in solar-powered technologies that have made them much more efficient and have cut costs. In recent years, architects and engineers have been designing many types of "green" buildings. These are not only more energy efficient, but they also incorporate a greater number of **passive solar** strategies for heating and cooling. In addition, thermal solar systems can be used to heat buildings and make hot water. Studies have shown that structures that have these innovations installed in them right from the start cost about the same as standard buildings. Then, not only do they use less energy, and therefore reduce fossil fuel emissions, but they also cost less to operate in the long run. It's a win-win situation.

In recent years the biggest improvements on the solar front have come in the area of generating electricity using the sun. There are two ways that this can be done. In a **concentrating solar power** system (CSP), hundreds of large mirrors called *heliostats* focus sunlight onto a central boiler, which creates steam to turn a generator. Although tests of these systems show that they work very well, the downside is that they are physically huge installations requiring a great deal of space and lots of sunlight. For the most part, these types of installations are best suited for desert areas such as the southwestern part of the United States.

A second, smaller-scale approach is to use **photovoltaic (PV)** systems, which directly convert sunlight to electricity. These are the

Figure 5.4 The eSolar Sierra SunTower power plant in Lancaster, California, in the Mojave Desert lies approximately 70 miles (110 km) north of Los Angeles. eSolar's concentrated solar power (CSP) system uses 24,000 mirrors, called heliostats, to reflect solar heat to a thermal receiver mounted atop two towers. Electrical power is produced when the focused heat boils water within the thermal receiver and produces steam, which is then piped to a nearby reconditioned 1947 GE turbine generator to produce electricity.

same types of devices used to power the international space station and portable electronic devices, such as solar-powered calculators. As with wind turbines, solar panels, as they are usually called, have been in active use for more than 30 years. The reason that these systems didn't immediately take off is that in the past, they were not very efficient at converting sunlight to electricity. Therefore the cost was high compared to the amount of power they produced. In addition, most of these systems were originally designed to be standalone structures, so they were mostly used to make electricity for structures that were located far away from power lines.

In the last 10 years the cost of installing PV systems has dropped tremendously. Now they are much more price-competitive with other means of generating electricity. In addition, most of the new systems are designed to be *grid-tied*, meaning that when they are installed, they are connected to the power lines that are operated by utility companies. This eliminates the need for batteries to store the

Figure 5.5   Solar roofs top the Solarsiedlung am Schlierberg solar settlement in Freiburg, Germany. These row houses, designed by solar architect Rolf Disch and completed in 2006, are "plus-energy" houses, meaning that they produce more energy than they consume.

electricity, which greatly reduces the system costs. On cloudy days, when the solar-powered system is not producing enough electricity, the extra energy comes from the utility company. Through a process called **net metering**, utilities must buy back extra electricity that is generated by the PV system when they are producing more electricity than is being used.

Perhaps the biggest advantage of small-scale PV systems is that they can be installed right onto the roof of an existing building. They can also be used to cover parking garages, warehouses, and other structures that would normally be considered wasted space. One of the most exciting developments in the past few years is the building of *integrated solar systems*. In these designs, special roofing tiles with the solar cells built right into them are used instead of standard shingles or tiles. Then there is no need to put a solar power system on a roof because the solar power system *is* the roof.

TRANSPORTATION FUELS

The transportation sector is extremely dependent on fossil fuels. Most of the energy used to run boats, trains, planes, cars, and trucks comes from oil and, to a lesser extent, natural gas. The biggest problem with converting the transportation sector to renewable energy is the fact that the fuel sources must be easily transported without adding too much weight to the vehicle. Also, since the engines found in most vehicles are designed to run on a liquid, any replacement fuel should be in a fluid state. There are a few things that are being done to make the transportation sector less dependent on oil.

One of the most important measures that governments can take is to raise the efficiency standards of cars and trucks. Simply by increasing the number of miles that a car or truck can go on a gallon of fuel will save a tremendous amount of greenhouse gases. One of the most effective ways of doing this is to build more hybrid cars, which have a small gasoline engine that charges a battery. The car itself then runs on electricity.

Another solution is to have all-electric vehicles that can be periodically recharged using electricity generated from renewable sources. In the past this was a problem because the batteries

Figure 5.6 The Chevy Volt is featured at the Annual Chicago Auto Show on February 15, 2011 in Chicago.

that powered the electric motor were big, heavy, and quickly ran down. Newer battery designs, thanks mainly to developments in cell phones and other portable electronic devices, are solving this problem. It won't be long before many new all-electric vehicles hit the roads.

Another way of reducing dependence on oil is to increase the use of **biofuels**, which are made from plants and other organic materials. The main biofuel currently in use is ethanol, which is a type of alcohol. In the United States today, 10% of the fuel sold at gasoline pumps is really ethanol. The blend can be easily increased to 20% without having to make any major adjustments to car engines. When it is burned, alcohol releases far fewer greenhouse gases than either gasoline or diesel fuel.

The problem lies in making it. Most of the ethanol made in the world today comes from either corn or sugar. Growing and processing these crops into fuel is a very energy-intensive process. Some scientific studies have shown that if you consider all of the energy used in the process of making ethanol, you use more energy than you get out of the fuel. At least for the present time, increasing ethanol use may not be a good alternative. Chemists are working on new ways of making biofuels. Most feel that it will be only a matter of time before a suitable substitute is available.

Cellulosic Ethanol

In addition to requiring a great deal of energy to produce it, another major drawback of ethanol as a transportation fuel is that it currently is made from plant materials that are potential food sources. Sugar from either sugar cane or sugar beets, and especially corn, are valuable food resources. Given the fact that a large portion of the world's population is already suffering from malnutrition, there is a real moral issue with using these resources to power cars. Because of the increased demand for ethanol, the price of corn in recent years has risen significantly. This may be good news for the farmers who grow it, but for the average person, any cost increase just makes food harder to get.

In an effort to solve this part of the problem, biochemists have been working on ways of making ethanol from non-food sources. In theory, alcohol can be made from cellulose, which is the main material that makes up plant cells. The problem with cellulose is that even though it contains the elements carbon, hydrogen, and oxygen, from which alcohol is made, it has a very rigid cell structure. This makes it very tough to break down. Standard means of distilling it don't work. Lab tests using other chemical processes, including bacteria and enzymes, have shown some promising results. If these processes can be scaled up into a working technology, then instead of using corn and sugar, producers of ethanol will be able to use wood chips, grass clippings, and other plant waste products to make the fuel.

CHANGING LAND USE PATTERNS

Cutting greenhouse gas emissions by reducing fossil fuel use will only solve one part of the global warming problem. A second issue comes from changing land use. When people cut down forests to raise crops and cattle, or clear open space to build cities and roads, they are also increasing the amount of carbon dioxide in the air. They are removing the "sinks" where carbon has been naturally stored.

During the past 20 years, many governments and conservation organizations have been working hard to try to stop the destruction of rainforests and other critically important, undeveloped areas. Unfortunately, trees are still falling at a record pace. The problem really comes down to economics. People need resources to live. In many countries, forests are the only means of getting those resources. When politicians and other concerned individuals in industrialized nations point at developing nations and say that they need to stop cutting down trees, the people in those nations quickly point back and say that countries in Europe and North America did the same thing 200 years ago. In addition, many of the resources that are being taken from the rainforests are being sold to people in industrialized nations so they can maintain their high standard of living.

The trick to saving the forests of the world is to somehow place an economic value on the living trees. The value must be greater than what the tree would be worth when it is cut down. This is the idea behind a program called REDD, which stands for Reducing Emissions from Deforestation and Forest Degradation. In theory, a successful REDD program could offset as much greenhouse gas emissions as is currently being produced by the entire global transportation sector.

Essentially, the way a REDD program would work is that forest managers would be rewarded for *not* cutting all their trees. Instead, they would only selectively cut certain trees, keeping the bulk of the forest intact. In addition, when they did remove trees, they would replace them with a similar species. This way the forest ecosystem would be able to continue with only a minimum amount of harm.

A financial incentive program such as REDD is a major improvement over just telling people to stop cutting trees. The question is where will the money come from to pay people for not cutting down trees? The mechanism that is most often discussed is generally referred to as *carbon cap and trade*, or **emissions trading**.

Here's how it might work: A government or inter-government agency sets a specific limit (or a *cap*) on how much carbon emissions a particular polluter can release into the air. This is similar to the idea behind the Kyoto Protocol. The carbon emission cap is considered to be the "allowable" amount, and the agency then issues "carbon credits" equaling this amount. As long as the polluter stays under the cap, it is fine. If it exceeds the cap, it must either reduce emissions to stay under the cap, or find another polluter who is not polluting as much and purchase enough carbon credits from it to equal the extra emissions.

For example, say two companies both have an emissions cap of 20 tons of CO_2 per year. That means they both have 20 carbon credits. Company A only emits 16 tons of CO_2, so it has 4 carbon credits left. Company B emits 22 tons of CO_2, so it must either reduce its emissions or, instead, it can buy 2 carbon credits from Company A to stay at the limit.

Since trees in a rainforest store carbon, managers of those trees would also receive carbon credits based on how many trees they keep standing. They could then sell the carbon credits to other companies. If they decide instead to cut the trees, they would lose the credits. If people were to take some open ground and start planting trees, they would get carbon credits they could sell. In this way, people would be encouraged not only to protect the forests that they have, but also to expand forests so that they would absorb and store more greenhouse gases.

Of course, as with any system this complex, there will be lots of problems. Someone has to regulate and enforce the trading of caps and someone has to make sure that the trees are still standing. On a positive note, emission-trading programs have worked on a limited basis in the past in the United States. The programs have been credited with helping to reduce acid precipitation and nitrous oxide emissions. However, even if a carbon cap and trade program were put into action in the next year, the results would take a while to see. Regardless, many political leaders and climate scientists feel that this type of program offers the only fair and workable solution to cutting greenhouse gases in the future.

GEOENGINEERING

What if after a few years, scientists discover that a cap and trade program isn't working as well as they had first believed it would? Even worse, what if it never comes about? Is there any other technological fix to help cool the planet in a hurry? Maybe. The process of using high-tech tools to change Earth's natural environment is called **geoengineering**. Although it may sound like science fiction to some people, there are a number of legitimate climate scientists who are looking into it as a possible, temporary measure to quickly cool the planet while waiting for other long-term solutions to take effect.

Some ideas, such as sending giant orbiting mirrors into space to reflect some of the sunlight away from the planet, are just too challenging. Others, such as dumping huge amounts of fertilizer into the oceans to get algae to grow and soak up more CO_2, would cause other environmental disasters that may be worse than global warming. Unfortunately, as of right now, there are no mammoth scrubbers to suck pollutants out of the air. There are, nevertheless, a few serious ideas offered by scientists as possible, temporary solutions that could quickly cool the planet.

Currently the most promising idea involves a process called "doping" the stratosphere. It mimics a natural process that happens with large volcanoes. After the eruption of Mt. Pinatubo, Earth's temperature cooled slightly for a few years. This happened because during the eruption tiny particles of volcanic ash were blasted high into the atmosphere. High-altitude winds then carried the particles around the globe. Once in the air, the particles scattered sunlight before it could reach the ground. This reduced the amount of solar radiation reaching Earth's surface.

In the geoengineering solution, tiny particles made from sulfur compounds would be set loose in the stratosphere, where they would basically act in the same way as particles from natural volcanic sources. Many climate scientists recognize that this process of "global dimming" is already happening due to aerosols found in air pollution. The 2007 Assessment Report of the IPCC states: "It is likely that greenhouse gases would have caused more warming than is currently observed if not for the cooling effects of volcanic and human-caused aerosols." What's not clear is how to get the particles into the air. Some suggestions include using hoses attached to high-altitude balloons, high-altitude planes with sprayers, and even artillery shells shot into the sky.

Of course, before any wide-scale use of aerosols can be undertaken, a great many tests must be done. Also, the risks of geoengineering are enormous. Even experimenting with it could create disasters. For example, it is quite possible that the particles used to block sunlight might also damage the ozone layer. Another problem is that altering the stratosphere could change precipitation patterns on Earth, causing extreme droughts and reducing food supplies. Clearly, when it comes to geoengineering, there are many more questions than answers.

Future Predictions

When it comes to predicting the future of Earth's climate, it's a little like trying to pick the winner of a horse race. There are some favorites, but every once in a while a long shot comes in to take the prize. The only thing known for certain is that change will happen. How fast these changes occur and how severe they will be is a really big question.

Based on the fossil record alone, scientists know that Earth has gone through periods when it has been both warmer and colder than it is right now. Using proxy data, climate scientists have been able to piece together the climate history since the last ice age. Even this has a great deal of uncertainty and shows some pretty significant variations in both temperature and moisture. The major wild card in all of this is the fact that the levels of greenhouse gases in the atmosphere are higher than they have been for quite some time, and there really isn't any data in the recent past with which to compare it.

CLIMATE MODELS

The best that climate scientists can offer are several different scenarios developed using a variety of different climate models. Unlike physical models of cars or planes, climate models are really nothing more than sophisticated computer programs that use mathematical formulas to make certain predictions based on the data that is fed into them. Most climate models belong to a type of program called a **GCM**, which stands for **general circulation model**. GCMs are designed to simulate the movement of the air in the atmosphere, the water in the ocean, and the interactions between the two. Most of the current models break Earth into individual cells, much like a digital camera breaks an image into individual pixels. In the case of a photograph, the smaller and more numerous the pixels, the higher the resolution and the sharper the image produced by the camera.

Because Earth is so large and there is so much data to account for, the individual cells in the GCMs are relatively large. Most cells are based on longitude and latitude and are usually set to be about 5 degrees in size. If you take a look at a map of the world, you'll see that a 5-degree square is enormous. At the equator, 1 degree of either latitude or longitude is about 69 miles (110 km) long. This means that a cell that is 5 degrees on a side can be almost 120,000 square miles (310,800 km) in size. That's almost 100 times larger than the state of Rhode Island. (It is important to note that this is a maximum value because lines of longitude get closer together as they move toward the poles.)

As a result of the huge size of cells, even the best climate models are going to have averaging errors. When climate models are run backwards in time in order to match them up with actual climate records of the past, data for individual cells often don't match the historical data for a specific location.

If climate models have these errors built into them from the start, you may be wondering why climate scientists even bother to use them at all. The main use of GCMs is to see how different climate factors control different outcomes. They are not really meant to predict the future. Even with their flaws, climate models provide extremely useful information and allow scientists to set certain limits based on different conditions and assumptions. Researchers using several different climate models with different programs have pretty much reached the same conclusion: Earth is warming quickly, and human activity is probably the cause.

In its 2007 assessment report, the IPCC offered several different predictions for the end of this century based on data from what they term "high" and "low" scenarios. Under the low scenario, the best estimate is that the likely temperature increase will be between 2.0 and 5.2°F (1.1 and 2.9°C). This will result in a sea level rise of between 7 and 15 inches (18 and 38 cm). With the high scenario, things would get much worse. The temperature increase would be between 4.3 and 11.5°F (2.4 and 6.4°C) and sea level rise would be between 10 and 23 inches (26 and 59 cm). If this were to happen, many of the world's major coastal cities, including New York and Miami, would be under water.

Uncertainties Abound

One of the things that climate deniers love to point out about climate models is that weather is considered to be a chaotic system, and chaotic systems are not predictable. This is actually true. Anybody who has ever planned an event based on a sunny five-day forecast, only to have it get rained out, knows that long-term weather predictions are almost impossible to make. But climate is not the same thing as weather. Even though some of the same factors, such as temperature and precipitation, are measured, changes in a regional climate operate much more slowly and are much easier to predict.

Another point that is often made against climate models is that back in the 1970s, many scientists were predicting that the next ice age was right around the corner. Back then, global cooling was the real concern. This is also true, but in the 1970s, the amount of data that scientists had to work with concerning global circulation patterns was a tiny fraction of what is available today. In addition, the computers and the models that they ran were dinosaurs compared to the supercomputers that are at work today. Comparing the two is like comparing the Wright Brothers' airplane with an F-16 fighter jet.

In defense of the global warming skeptics, it is important to note that there are still many uncertainties concerning the mechanisms of climate change that probably have not been accounted for. As a result, even the most likely scenarios may be seriously flawed. Most climate scientists admit this freely. Some of the most pressing questions that have climate scientists concerned include: What role will methane gas escaping melting permafrost play in speeding up global warming? How fast will the ice sheets on Antarctica and Greenland melt? What will happen to cloud cover as temperatures warm and

Concerns About Black Carbon

Aerosols in the atmosphere help cool the planet through a process called *global dimming*. By reflecting and scattering sunlight before it reaches Earth's surface, these tiny particles are thought to reduce the amount of radiant energy the planet receives. The concept forms the backbone of many geoengineering plans to cool the planet. Unfortunately, based on some new scientific findings, it appears that all aerosols don't work the same way. One big question that only recently has been raised is what role **black carbon** plays in either warming or cooling the atmosphere.

Black carbon, which most of us simply refer to as soot, are aerosols that come from the burning of fossil fuels and wood fires. Because they are so small and light, they tend to stay suspended in the air for a long time. The albedo effect causes different objects to either reflect or absorb light energy. Because soot particles are black, instead of reflecting and scattering light like sulfur aerosols do, they have a very low albedo and tend to absorb solar radiation. As a result, black carbon particles may be acting to warm the atmosphere directly. Atmospheric scientists are currently conducting research on how big of a role black carbon plays in the global warming process. Depending on what they discover, they may have to rewrite the equations for Earth's energy balance.

there is more water vapor in the air? Will the ocean circulation patterns that we now have stop or change direction?

COPENHAGEN AND CANCUN

Given the uncertainties that remain about the impacts of global warming, it's not surprising that climate scientists are having a hard time reaching an agreement about what the next course of action should be. Political leaders have an even tougher job because in addition to having to deal with the science, they also have to protect the best interests of their own countries and people. It has been more than a decade since the Kyoto Protocol was first agreed upon, and very little tangible action has been taken since then.

In 2009, climate delegates from all over the world met in Copenhagen, Denmark, to hammer out a binding agreement to cut greenhouse gas emissions. The result was a disaster. After the meetings, many people called for the end of the UNFCCC. Instead of giving up, the climate delegates returned to the bargaining table in December 2010 in Cancun, Mexico. To their credit, they were able to reach some common ground in what is known as the Cancun Agreement.

Unlike the Kyoto Protocol, which set greenhouse gas emission limits on only industrialized countries, this new agreement commits both developed and developing countries (including China and India) to take climate action that will be "transparent and measurable." Unfortunately, the Cancun Agreement still does not set binding emission limits on countries. It is hoped that this will come in the next series of meetings in 2011. Still, it does show that the people in power are taking global warming seriously. Once people agree that the problem exists, it's only a matter of time before the solutions will follow. Let's just hope that the solutions arrive before the impacts from global warming become too great to reverse.

Glossary

aerosols   Tiny particles in the air that reflect sunlight back into space and form clouds

albedo   The relative reflectivity of an object or surface

anthropogenic   Made by humans

atmosphere   The mass of air surrounding Earth

biofuel   A fuel such as ethanol that is used to replace petroleum products

black carbon   Aerosols commonly called "soot" that absorb sunlight and heat the air directly

carbon cycle   The process in which carbon atoms get recycled through the atmosphere and living things on Earth

carbon footprint   The amount of greenhouse gases generated by a person or group of people

climate   The long-term average of weather conditions for a given region

concentrating solar power (CSP)   A system using mirrors to concentrate sunlight on a boiler, creating steam to run an electric generator

convection   The process in which heat gets transferred through a fluid, such as water or air

Coriolis effect   The bending of wind and water currents in the ocean due to Earth's rotation

dendrochronology   The technique of using tree ring data to date past events and determine past climate conditions

El Niño Southern Oscillation (ENSO) A climate disruption that happens on a periodic basis in the area around the southern Pacific Ocean

electromagnetic spectrum The total range of energy in different wavelengths coming from the Sun. The spectrum includes radio waves, infrared light, visible light, ultraviolet light, X-rays, and gamma rays.

emissions trading Also called "cap and trade," this system allows polluters to buy "credits" from those nations or companies that do not pollute as much

fluid A liquid or gas that is able to flow under a force or pressure.

fossil fuel An energy source made from ancient living things; oil, natural gas, and coal are all fossil fuels.

general circulation model (GCM) A computer model used to simulate climate changes on Earth under different conditions

geoengineering The process of using large-scale technology to change a portion of Earth's environment

glacial period A stage of global cooling when continental ice sheets covered much of the planet; it is commonly called an "ice age."

greenhouse effect The process in which heat energy is trapped on one side of a semi-transparent barrier, such as the glass in a greenhouse or certain gases in the atmosphere

greenhouse gases A gas such as carbon dioxide or methane that acts to trap heat in the troposphere and raise the surface temperature of the planet.

heat island The localized heating that happens around cities and other large structures where concrete absorbs sunlight and re-radiates it as heat

hydroelectric Relating to the production of energy by water-power

interglacial stage The period in between glacial stages or ice ages when ice sheets melt and temperatures warm

Intergovernmental Panel on Climate Change (IPCC) A body of scientists working under the guidelines set up by the UN to study the effects of global warming and make recommendations for actions to be taken

isotope   One of several forms that the atom of an element can take

microclimate   A localized climate controlled by specific factors, such as a warm ocean current or the presence of a nearby mountain range

North Atlantic Oscillation (NAO)   A climate disruption that happens on a periodic basis in the area around the northern Atlantic Ocean

net metering   A system in which utilities must buy back electrical power generated by an independent source, such as a homeowner with a PV system

ozone   A naturally forming gas molecule found in the atmosphere, consisting of three oxygen atoms (O_3)

ozone layer   A layer in the stratosphere that contains a high concentration of ozone molecules. It protects Earth's surface from ultraviolet radiation coming from the Sun.

paleoclimatology   The study of ancient climates using proxy data such as ice cores, sediment cores, fossils, and tree rings.

passive solar   A solar system that uses glass, insulation, and mass to capture and store heat energy; it usually has few, if any, moving parts.

permafrost   Permanently frozen soil found in polar regions, often containing trapped methane gas

photovoltaic (PV)   An electrical generating system that uses solar cells to directly convert light energy to electricity

proxy   Something that stands in for something or someone else; proxy climate data include things such as tree rings, ice cores, fossil pollen, and sediment cores.

radiant energy   Radiation that is directly transmitted and absorbed; the Sun sends out radiant energy in the form of electromagnetic waves, including visible light.

solar constant   The average energy output of the Sun; while it does vary slightly, it generally stays within a narrow range.

specific heat   The measurement of how fast or slow a substance will heat up or cool down; it also measures how much heat energy a substance can store.

stratosphere   The second layer of the atmosphere, ranging from 6 to 30 miles (10 to 48 km) above Earth's surface. The stratosphere contains the ozone layer.

thermal expansion   The process in which matter expands when it is heated

transpiration   The process in which plants release water vapor from their leaves into the surrounding air

troposphere   The lowest level of the atmosphere, where most weather changes occur

ultraviolet radiation   Invisible form of electromagnetic radiation that has a shorter wavelength than visible light

weather   The day-to-day changes in air temperature, wind conditions, humidity, and precipitation occurring in a local area

wind turbine   A windmill used to generate electricity

Bibliography

Ahrens, C. Donald. *Meteorology Today: An Introduction to Weather, Climate, and the Environment.* 7th ed. Pacific Grove, Calif.: Thomson Brooke/Cole, 2003.

Aron, Joan L., and Jonathan A. Patz. *Ecosystem Change and Public Health.* Baltimore: The Johns Hopkins University Press, 2001.

Broecker, Wallace S. and Robert Kunzig. *Fixing Climate.* New York: Hill and Wang, 2008.

Easton, Thomas A. *Taking Sides: Clashing Views on Controversial Issues in Science, Technology and Society.* 5th ed. Guilford, Conn.: McGraw-Hill/Dushkin, 2002.

Goodell, Jeff. *How to Cool the Planet.* Boston: Houghton Mifflin Harcourt, 2010.

Harris, Stewart. *Pollution and Human Health.* New York: Wiley Custom Services, 2004.

Intergovernmental Panel on Climate Change. IPCC Fourth Assessment Report (Climate Change 2007) Web site. Available online. URL: http://www.ipcc.ch.

LePage, Michael. "Climate Change: A guide for the perplexed" Web site. Available online. URL: http://www.newscientist.com/article/dn11462-climate-change-a-guide-for-the-perplexed.htm.

Linden, Eugene. *The Winds of Change.* New York: Simon and Schuster, 2006.

Nadakavukaren, Anne. *Our Global Environment.* 5th ed. Prospect Heights, Ill.: Waveland Press, 2000.

IPCC Report. "The Arctic: Thawing Permafrost, Melting Sea Ice, and More Significant Changes." Science Daily Web site. April 11, 2007. Available online. URL: http://www.sciencedaily.com/releases/2007/04/070410140922.htm.

United Nations Framework Convention on Climate Change (Kyoto Protocol) Web site. Available online. URL: http://unfcc.int/kyoto_protocol/items/2830txt.php.

U.S. Energy Information Administration Web site. "2010 International Energy Outlook." Available online. URL: http://www.eia.doe.gov/oiaf/ieo/world.html.

U.S. Environmental Protection Agency Web site. "Cap and Trade." Available online. URL: http://www.epa.gov/capandtrade.

Witze, Alexandra. "The Final Climate Frontiers." *Science News* 178, no. 12 (December 4, 2010).

Further Resources

Calhoun, Yael, (Series Editor) *Environmental Issues: Climate Change.* Philadelphia: Chelsea House, 2005.

Gaughen, Shasta. (ed.) *Global Warming: Contemporary Issues Companion.* Detroit: Greenhaven Press, 2005.

Goodell, Jeff. *How to Cool the Planet.* Boston: Houghton Mifflin Harcourt, 2010.

Gore, Al. *An Inconvenient Truth: The Planetary Emergency of Global Warming and What We Can Do About It.* Emmaus, Penn.: Rodale, 2006.

Green, Kenneth. *Global Warming: Understanding the Debate.* Berkeley Heights, N.J.: Enslow Publishers, 2002.

Miller, Debra A. (ed.) *Global Warming.* Detroit: Greenhaven Press, 2008.

Robinson, Matthew. *America Debates Global Warming: Crisis or Myth?* New York: The Rosen Publishing Group, 2008.

Web Sites

Intergovernmental Panel on Climate Change (IPCC)
http://www.ipcc.ch
> *Read the latest assessment report on global warming and get the latest predictions on the impacts of climate change.*

Nature Conservancy
http://nature.org
> *Discover how you can be part of the solution in saving rainforests. Includes a personal carbon footprint calculator.*

National Oceanic and Atmospheric Administration (NOAA)
http://www.noaa.gov
> *Get the latest updates on weather and climate from the U.S. government's primary source for information on the oceans and atmosphere.*

Pew Center on Global Climate Change

www.pewclimate.org

> *This site provides unbiased information on climate change and its possible impact on society.*

Union of Concerned Scientists (UCS)

http://www.ucsusa.org

> *Learn more about the science behind global warming and some of the possible solutions.*

United States Environmental Protection Agency (EPA)

http://www.epa.gov

> *Learn about the different regulations concerning atmospheric gases and how different emission cap and trade programs work.*

United Nations Convention on Climate Change (UNFCCC)

http://unfccc.int

> *Get the details on the first international treaty dealing with climate change, including the latest information about the Kyoto Protocol.*

World Meteorological Organization (WMO)

http://www.wmo.int

> *This site offers links to technical reports on climate change as well as the latest weather and climate conditions around the planet.*

Picture Credits

Index

About the Author

Stephen M. Tomecek is a geologist and science educator who has written more than 30 science books for children, young adults, and teachers. He earned his bachelor's degree with honors in earth and environmental sciences from Queens College of the City University of New York, after which he spent three years working as an environmental planner for the Westchester County Soil and Water Conservation District in New York State. Since 1989, he has served as the executive director of Science Plus, a company that provides science enrichment programs and staff development workshops for schools and museums throughout the United States. He also serves as a science consultant and writer for the National Geographic Society and Scholastic, and is an active member of the Union of Concerned Scientists. His 1996 book *Bouncing & Bending Light* won the American Institute of Physics Science Writing Award.

Dedication and Acknowledgment

Dedication

This book is in honor of Dr. Barry Commoner, whose groundbreaking books *Science and Survival* and *The Closing Circle* inspired me to become a scientist and work for a better environment, and for Dr. Jonathan Patz, Director of the Program on Health Effects of Global Environmental Change at the Johns Hopkins School of Public Health, who first alerted me to the severity of the global warming problem.

Acknowledgement

I would like to thank Dr. Todd Ellis, Associate Professor of Meteorology at the State University of New York College at Oneonta for taking the time to meet with me and give me a clearer picture of the climate change debate. I would also like to thank Father John Monaghan of Cardinal Spellman High School in New York City for supplying me with a number of important resources that proved to be valuable assets in researching this book.